THE MODERN MEDALLION WORKBOOK

11 Designers Share Quilt Projects to Make, Mix & Match

Janice Zeller Ryan and Beth Vassalo

stashBOOKS.
an imprint of C&T Publishing

Text copyright © 2015 by Janice Zeller Ryan and Beth Vassalo

Photography and artwork copyright © 2015 by C&T Publishing, Inc.

Publisher: Amy Marson

Creative Director: Gailen Runge

Art Director: Kristy Zacharias

Editors: Lynn Koolish and Katie Van Amburg

Technical Editors: Alison M. Schmidt and Helen Frost

Cover/Book Designer: April Mostek

Production Coordinator: Jenny Davis

Production Editor: Joanna Burgarino

Illustrator: Wendy Mathson

Photo Assistant: Mary Peyton Peppo

Photography by Diane Pedersen, unless otherwise noted

Published by Stash Books, an imprint of C&T Publishing, Inc., P.O. Box 1456, Lafayette, CA 94549

Library of Congress Cataloging-in-Publication Data

Ryan, Janice Zeller, 1974-

 The modern medallion workbook : 11 designers share quilt projects to make, mix & match / Janice Zeller Ryan and Beth Vassalo.

   pages cm

 ISBN 978-1-60705-991-2 (soft cover)

1. Quilting--Patterns. 2. Patchwork--Patterns. 3. Patchwork quilts. 4. Medallions (Decorative arts) I. Vassalo, Beth, 1971- II. Title.

 TT835.R926 2015

 746.46--dc23

                          2014036816

Printed in China

10 9 8 7 6 5 4 3 2 1

Dedication

From Janice

To JD for making this book possible. To Liam and Emmeline for being my biggest (and tiniest) fans. To my parents for always supporting my crazy, artistic endeavors.

From Beth

To M for inspiring me to start sewing and continuing to inspire me with your innovation and resourcefulness. To E for being my constant companion at the sewing machine and for challenging and encouraging me to try new things. To T for keeping me laughing (as only a two-year-old can). To N and A for their support. To P for being there so this all could happen.

Acknowledgments

We would like to extend our gratitude to everyone who made this book possible, including all of the wonderful pattern contributors, our editors, C&T, and of course, our loving families. Thank you!

CONTENTS

PREFACE

Neither of us could have imagined when we first met in 2012 that we would soon be collaborating on a book about quilting. We met the same way that many modern quilters meet these days—through our quilting blogs. We were soon communicating daily, not only about quilting but also about life in general. During the summer of 2013, we were each individually working on ideas for a quilting book. We chatted about it often, and then one day we thought: Wouldn't it be fun to write a book together?

This conversation took place at the same time that the quilting world was introduced to *Marcelle Medallion* by Alexia Marcelle Abegg, from her book *Liberty Love*.

Marcelle Medallion by Alexia Marcelle Abegg

BETH

Janice had been working on designs for a medallion quilt and suggested that as the topic for our book. I was hesitant, though—don't medallion quilts require perfect precision, planning, and accuracy? That was not exactly my style of quilt-making. We talked about other ideas, but Janice kept bringing back the idea of a book about modern medallions. I was thinking that maybe we should go back to each writing our own book proposals, but then late one night, a design idea came to me. It was one of those times when you have to get out of bed and write it down so you don't forget. It was a lightbulb moment for me when I realized that the definition of a medallion quilt is just a quilt made up of borders surrounding a center medallion—nowhere in that definition does it state that they have to be equal, perfect, or matched. I drew my design and emailed it to Janice, along with a note saying, "Yes, let's write a book about modern medallions."

JANICE

From the moment Beth and I first discussed it, I was seriously excited and invested in the idea of a medallion book. I love a challenge, and I get a thrill out of teaching people new techniques that expand their sewing universe. A medallion is the perfect canvas for quiltmakers to learn new skills and become comfortable deviating from a written project to find their own style. It's a sort of sampler quilt in the round. I was very happy when Beth finally "came 'round" and agreed to the book concept. Although we are both modern quilters, our design tastes and our sewing styles are very different, which helps us write for a variety of quilters.

We spent the next several days thinking more and more about the idea and getting more excited with each email we sent. Through these conversations, we realized that we wanted the book to include a unique, varied selection of medallion quilts from a diverse group of quilt designers and that we wanted the book to be more than just projects. We wanted it to be a resource for all quilters wanting to design their own modern medallion quilts. As such, it would include information for resizing and modifying borders to create unique quilts by mixing and matching the elements from the book's projects. We also wanted to include detailed instructions and information for piecing the more popular designs used in medallion quilts. Several emails later, the idea for *The Modern Medallion Workbook* was born—a book that includes eleven complete projects in a variety of styles and the tools and inspiration to help you, the reader, build your own modern medallion quilt.

Introduction

A medallion quilt is simply defined as a quilt composed of a center motif surrounded by multiple borders. This style of quilting was brought to America in the late 1700s by the colonists emigrating from Europe. These medallion quilts (referred to as *framed quilts* in Europe) included both symmetrical and asymmetrical styles and were made using many techniques, from simple patchwork to intricate piecing and appliqué. The center motifs in these early medallions were often made from either appliqué, wholecloth printed fabrics, or a pieced design. The borders were also pieced, appliquéd, or a combination of both. Some quilts had many borders, while others had just a few, allowing the center to remain the star.

Medallions remained a popular style of quilting until the 1840s, when many quiltmakers began using rows of blocks instead. In recent times, however, the medallion quilt has had a resurgence in the modern quilting movement. Although the definition of a medallion quilt remains the same, through the addition of modern fabrics and a modern aesthetic, this quilt has become increasingly popular with modern quilters. While there are many definitions of what makes a quilt modern, we believe it is a subjective test and that you decide whether a quilt is modern or traditional—or whether that distinction even matters.

Making a modern medallion quilt is a process, and we want you to enjoy every single step, just as we do. We encourage you to slow down, take your time, and embrace the creativity that goes into making a medallion quilt. Begin by mindfully choosing your fabrics and planning your design; we've even included line drawings that you can use as coloring pages to help with this (see Line Drawings of the Quilts, page 128). Don't rush this first step! Continue to enjoy the process with each new border—try a technique you've never tried before (remember, the seam ripper is your friend); challenge yourself. Your efforts will be rewarded when you see your modern medallion masterpiece!

PLANNING AND ORGANIZING
Your Modern Medallion Quilt

FABRIC CONSIDERATIONS

One of our favorite parts of starting a new project is selecting the fabrics. And making a modern medallion quilt provides lots of opportunity for fabric play.

You can decide the fabrics for your entire quilt all at once, or you can plan the quilt border by border. If you are going to select fabrics along the way, decide on an overall theme or color scheme at the beginning to keep the borders harmonious. One way to figure out a color palette is by selecting one piece of print fabric to inspire the rest of the selection. You don't have to be bound to the colors in that fabric or even use that fabric; instead you can use it as a guide to choose other fabrics that complement each other. Another option is to build the color palette by taking inspiration from a favorite photo, a piece of art, or any other object that is special to you.

If you decide on a scrappy look for your quilt, consider choosing fabrics with only a few colors in each print, as this will result in a less busy design when the fabrics are combined. When choosing fabrics, consider the size of the pieces you are cutting—if you choose a design with mostly small pieces, you might want to focus on small- and medium-scale print fabrics, since any large print will get lost when you chop it into small pieces.

TIP: Use Line Drawings of the Quilts (page 128) to experiment with different color choices and layouts for each quilt.

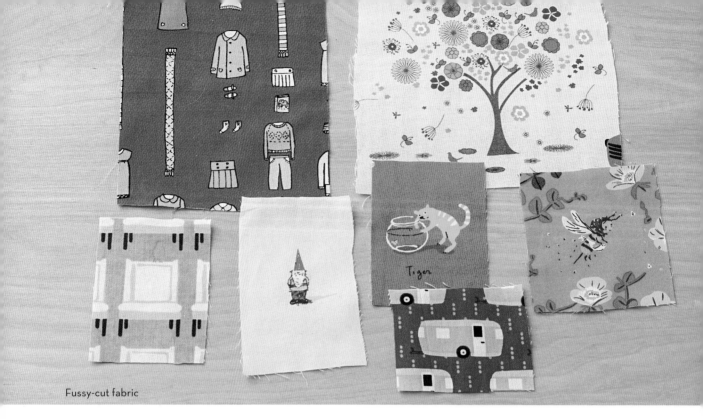

Fussy-cut fabric

Many of the medallion quilts in this book have at least one border that is made from strips of a single fabric. Consider your quilt's style and design when you are choosing what fabric to use for these borders. For some of the quilts, including one or more borders of plain solid fabric will work best, as it gives the eye a place to rest. For others—particularly those that contain a lot of negative space—using a print fabric, such as a chevron or a stripe, may enhance the overall look.

Another option is to fussy cut, which means to cut your fabric to highlight a specific design or portion of the fabric. Many of the modern medallion quilts in this book provide the perfect opportunity to fussy cut fabric. You can use pieces cut this way in your center motif, your corner blocks, or anywhere else you see fit.

Whatever fabric you use in your medallion, the most important thing is to give yourself whatever time you need to make a decision. This is not a step to rush through. Give yourself the opportunity to consider a variety of fabric combinations before committing.

DESIGN WALL

A design wall is an extremely helpful tool in planning and working on your medallion. You can make your design wall as simple or as complex as you want—just be sure that it is large enough to accommodate the finished size of your medallion.

> **TIP:** To make a simple, temporary design wall, just hang a large piece of cotton batting or flannel in a light neutral color on a wall.

A design wall allows you to see everything and easily change the placement of your fabrics before committing. If you are using a design wall that you cannot leave in place during the construction of your medallion (or if your design wall is the floor), be sure to take photos so you remember where you placed everything.

STAYING ORGANIZED

Most modern medallion quilts, including the projects in this book, contain a lot of pieces—pieces that you need to keep organized throughout the process. Some quilters prefer to do all of their cutting before they sew a single stitch, while others prefer to cut the pieces just for the current border. Whichever you decide, having a plan for organizing will eliminate future frustration. Whether you choose to organize using bins, piles, bags, or another method, be sure to liberally label so you know what goes where and when.

One way to organize projects

SEWING ORDER

When reading through the projects, you will notice that while some designers choose to attach borders to the quilt as soon as they are completed, others make all the borders first and sew everything together at the end. There is no right or wrong way to do this—it is a personal preference. If you attach the borders as they are completed, you will have the instant satisfaction of seeing your quilt come together. You will also be able to quickly correct any measuring mistakes if you have a border that does not fit as it should. However, if you wait until all the borders are completed before sewing them together, you will be able to see the quilt as a whole (a design wall really helps here) and switch out any borders or fabrics that aren't working.

> **IMPORTANT:** For some of the projects, you need to follow the order exactly as written by the designer. When this is the case, a note is included.

Regardless of which method you prefer, begin with the center medallion and work your way out, border by border. Measure as you go to make sure that your measurements are on track and that the next border will fit as written. If your borders end up measuring too large or too small, refer to Making a Border Fit (page 112).

> **NOTE:** Be sure to measure your quilt through the center and not along the edges, because the edges can stretch.

> **TIP:** Before you attach the borders, fold both the border and the quilt top in half and mark the centers of each edge with a pin. Place your quilt and borders flat on the table or floor to pin them together, matching the center pins. To reduce stretching and warping, do not let long pieces hang off the edge of a table. For larger quilts, fold the borders and quilt top in quarters, not just in half.

BREAK IT DOWN

When you look through the projects, some medallion quilts may seem too overwhelming and time consuming with all the cutting and organizing and measuring. If it seems overwhelming as a whole, just think about the quilt one border at a time. The line drawings of the quilts (page 128) will be especially helpful if you choose to do this, as they will help you plan your quilt and give you a reference guide that you can use over several days (or weeks or even months) so that you can pace yourself. Constructing a modern medallion quilt should be a marathon, not a sprint!

TIP: Many of the quilts in this book are perfect to use for round robin quilting bees. In this type of bee, one person makes the center block and then passes it to a member who adds a border before passing it to another member, who adds the next border. The quilt is passed around until all the borders are finished. The members can decide on a color palette together, or the person who makes the center block can choose the palette and send pieces of some of the fabrics to the other members to use throughout the making so that the quilt will finish with a varied but cohesive look.

Make note of plans before starting medallion quilts.

Make It Yours

Medallion quilts provide a perfect opportunity for customization. You can mix and match the centers and borders from many of the projects in this book or even add your own. We have included several methods and formulas (Make It Yours, page 110) that you can use to personalize your medallion quilt.

FINISHING YOUR MEDALLION QUILT

Backing

You have many choices when it comes to designing the backing for your medallion quilt—use just one fabric, or piece together a simple or intricate design. Carry elements of the design from the front of the quilt by using leftover fabrics and blocks. Making the back can be as fun as making the front. Don't rush—embrace and enjoy it!

Quilting

There is definitely no "right" way to quilt a medallion quilt. This book shows a variety of quilting options that work well for medallion quilts, including quilts that showcase a different design for each border and quilts that use an allover design to connect the various elements.

Binding

For a medallion quilt, the binding can appear as the final border. Whether you choose a fabric used in the quilt top or introduce a new fabric into the mix, remember that the binding is a design element of your quilt. Use a fabric that complements, rather than distracts from, your quilt.

A FEW NOTES
Before You Get Started

CHECK YOUR SEAMS

All the projects in this book use a scant ¼″ seam for piecing unless otherwise noted. For many medallion quilts, the accuracy and consistency of your seam allowance is very important—a small discrepancy multiplied across many blocks can lead to borders that might not fit correctly. Check your seam allowance to ensure it is accurate. A scant ¼″ seam allowance means a thread or two less than ¼″. To test, cut 2 squares 2″ × 2″ and sew them together. Sewn together, they should measure exactly 3½″ across the seamed width.

Test ¼″ seam.

Some quilters find it best to purchase a ¼″ seam foot for their sewing machine (which you will still need to check for accuracy), or you can use painter's, masking, or washi tape to mark the perfect ¼″ on your sewing machine.

PRESSING SEAMS

Many of the project and technique instructions in this book include information about which direction to press your seams. When there are no specific instructions, just use your personal preference—pressing the seams open or pressing them toward the darker fabric. Just remember to press, not iron: gently press the iron on the fabric, lift, and repeat. Do not move the iron around, as that can distort the fabric.

While you may be tempted to skip this step or to press your seams less often than suggested, we want to encourage you to continually press your seams throughout the construction of your medallion quilt. You will be happy that you didn't skimp on pressing when you see your final result!

TIP: Be especially careful when pressing bias edges, as they stretch easily.

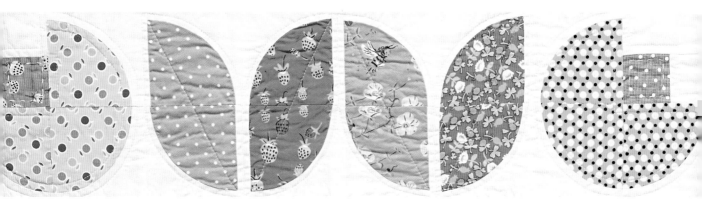

DON'T RUN OUT OF FABRIC

As the adage goes, measure twice, cut once. The fabric requirements listed in All Materials Needed for Quilt are all rounded up, but we strongly suggest that you buy more than you think you'll need—especially if you are using one background fabric throughout your quilt or for any plain borders. The border-by-border listings do not include as much extra for mistakes as the total amount given.

You don't want to get halfway through the making of your quilt and realize that because of a cutting error or a piecing mistake, you are a few inches short. Also, because you might be using some new-to-you techniques, you'll want to have extra fabric in case the first few blocks don't come out exactly the way you expect.

TIP: We also suggest that you use scraps to make a test block for new-to-you or difficult techniques.

Note: The cutting instructions for the included projects are based on fabrics that are at least 40″ wide (unless otherwise noted) after prewashing and removing the selvages.

SQUARING YOUR FABRIC

While all fabric needs to be squared and trimmed before quilting, we recommend that you pay close attention to this step for the projects in this book that rely on accurate cutting—especially for the plain borders. Fold your fabric in half lengthwise and line up the selvages exactly on top of each other. You will probably notice that the fold is not lying flat

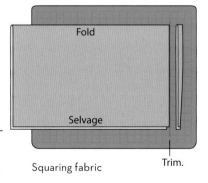

Fold

Selvage

Squaring fabric

Trim.

anymore. Keep your selvage edges lined up; then shift and smooth the fabric until the fold lies flat. Line up the fold of the fabric with the cutting mat grid. Then line up the ruler with the fold of the fabric and trim the raw edge using a rotary cutter. Now you are ready to cut your pieces.

TIP: After you square up your fabric, you may want to trim off the selvages. This will save time later.

CHAIN PIECING

Many of the projects in this book contain elements that are perfect for chain piecing, which is sewing together several matched pairs of fabric pieces in a row without stopping. To chain piece, cut your pieces according to the project instructions and place them right sides together as directed. Begin sewing the first pair of pieces. When you get to the edge of the fabric, sew a couple of stitches past that edge and then, without clipping the threads, place the next pair, sew, and repeat. After sewing through all the pairs, snip the threads.

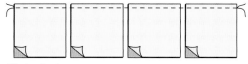

Chain piecing

PREWASHING

Whether you prewash your fabric is totally up to you. Prewashing removes the sizing and shrinks the fabric. It also reduces the chance that dark colors will bleed when the quilt is washed. The important thing is that if you decide to prewash your fabric, you will need to prewash *all* of the fabric in your quilt.

PINNING

Deciding whether or not to use pins is also a personal decision. However, this is definitely something to consider with a medallion quilt, especially as you get to the last borders. To keep the fabric from shifting when you sew, insert the pins perpendicular to the edge of the fabric. Remove the pins as you sew—do not sew over them, as doing so could damage your machine.

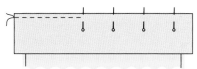

Pin perpendicular to edge and remove pins as you sew.

THE PROJECTS

On the following pages, you will find quilts designed and made by a group of designers. Some of the quilts are more on the traditional edge of modern quiltmaking, while others are very modern in style and design. Because we wanted each project designer's voice to come through with her project, you might notice some differences among the writing styles and instructions for the projects. Further, some of the designers prefer that you first piece the borders before constructing the medallion, while others instruct you to sew each border to the center or previous border before making the next one. Thus, we strongly recommend that you always read through the entire project before starting.

Each project is organized so that you can easily collect fabrics and make one border or, in the case of Zen Medallion (page 103), one wedge at a time. The projects begin by listing all the materials needed to make the quilt, including the amount of each fabric needed. The project is then broken up into a border-by-border listing of fabric requirements, and cutting and assembly instructions. The border-by-border listing of fabric requirements allows you to easily change the fabrics used for each border.

MIGRATION
MEDALLION

By Janice Zeller Ryan • Quilted by Angela Walters

The fabrics used in this quilt are Kona Cottons from Robert Kaufman.

I love the elaborate detail and varied fabrics of medallion quilts, but these features can also make the quilts appear quite heavy with pattern and color. My goal was to make a medallion quilt that was light and airy, yet still intricate. For Migration Medallion, the negative space, combined with the bright, solid colors, makes the borders and blocks appear to float and dance around the quilt. I chose the name Migration to evoke the images of movement and birds in coordinated flight.

—Janice

ALL MATERIALS NEEDED FOR QUILT

A variety of colors: 16 fat quarters for pieced borders

Solid-color scraps: a variety totaling 32 pieces, each at least 5″ × 8″, for center medallion (You can get some of these from the 16 fat quarters.)

4 different solid fabrics (green, aqua, and grays): 2⅜ yards total for borders 1–4, 6–8, and 10

Background: 4 yards

Binding: ½ yard

Backing: 4 yards

Batting: 69″ × 69″

Foundation paper, such as Carol Doak's Foundation Paper or Simple Foundations Translucent Vellum Paper (Legal size is helpful for Pattern C; otherwise you will need to tape smaller sheets together.)

Freezer paper or template plastic

FABRIC, CUTTING, AND CONSTRUCTION (BY BORDER)

Note: All seam allowances are ¼″. Refer to Foundation Paper Piecing (page 124) as needed.

Copy the patterns (pullout page P2) and cut them out to create Paper Foundations A, B, and C, and Cutting Templates D and E. You will need 4 foundation paper copies each of A, B, and C, and 1 template plastic or freezer paper copy each of D and E.

Note: Compare your copies with the original patterns to make sure they are exactly the same. If the patterns are at all different, you won't be able to sew the pieces together properly.

Center Medallion

Navy blue: 1 fat quarter

Variety of solids: at least a 5″ × 8″ scrap each of 32 colors (may be taken from fat quarters)

Background: 1 yard

CUT

Navy blue

- Cut 4 of Template D.

Variety of solids

- Cut 32 rectangles (1 of each color) roughly 2″ × 4″ for the pattern A and B triangles. (*Note: The triangles closer to the center will use less fabric. This measurement is the largest size you will need.*)

- Cut 32 rectangles (1 of each color) 2½″ × 3½″ for the pattern C circle of geese.

Background

- Cut 40 rectangles roughly 1½″ × 4″ for the pattern A and B background. (*Note: The triangles closer to the center will use less fabric. This measurement is the largest size you will need.*)

- Cut 8 rectangles 2″ × 7½″ for the pattern A and B background.

- Cut 64 rectangles 2¼″ × 3″ for the pattern C circle of geese background.

- Cut 4 of Template E.

SEW

1. Refer to Foundation Paper Piecing (page 124) to paper piece Foundations A, B, and C with the background and colored rectangles. Refer to the finished quilt photo (page 15) for color placement.

2. Remove the paper.

3. Sew A to B. Press the seams open.

4. Sew C to A/B (refer to Piecing Curves, page 117). Press the seams toward the center.

5. Sew D to A/B/C. Press the seams toward D.

6. Sew E to A/B/C/D. Press the seams toward D.

7. Repeat Steps 1–6 to make 3 more blocks. *Figure A*

8. Sew together the blocks in 2 rows of 2 to form a circle. Press the seams open.

9. Trim the center medallion to 21½″ × 21½″. *Figure B*

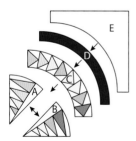

Figure A: Medallion block assembly

Figure B: Center medallion

Border 1

FABRIC

Gray: 1/3 yard

CUT

Gray

- Cut 2 strips 2½" × 21½".
- Cut 2 strips 2½" × 25½".

Border 2

FABRIC

Aqua: 1/8 yard

Background: 1 scrap

CUT

Aqua

- Cut 2 strips 1½" × 25½".
- Cut 2 strips 1½" × 15½".
- Cut 6 rectangles 1½" × 2½".

Background

- Cut 6 rectangles 1½" × 2½".

SEW

1. Sew 3 background and 3 aqua rectangles to a short end of the 1½" × 15½" aqua strip, alternating colors. Press the seams open.

2. Repeat Step 1 to create the second pieced border strip.

Border 2 assembly

Border 3

FABRIC

Background: 1/8 yard

Aqua: 1 scrap

CUT

Background

- Cut 2 strips 1½" × 27½".
- Cut 2 strips 1½" × 16½".
- Cut 4 rectangles 1½" × 2½".
- Cut 2 rectangles 1½" × 3½".

Aqua

- Cut 6 rectangles 1½" × 2½".

SEW

1. Sew 2 background and 3 aqua 1½" × 2½" rectangles to the short end of the 1½" × 16½" background strip, alternating colors. Press the seams open.

2. Sew the remaining 1½" × 3½" rectangle to the end of the strip. Press the seam open.

3. Repeat Steps 1 and 2 to create the second strip.

Border 3 assembly

Border 4

FABRIC

Green: 1/4 yard

CUT

Green

- Cut 2 strips 2" × 29½".
- Cut 2 strips 2" × 32½".

Border 5

FABRIC

Background: 3/4 yard

Light red, yellow, green, and blue: 1/8 yard each or from fat quarters

Dark red, yellow, green, and blue: 1/8 yard each or from fat quarters

CUT

Background

- Cut 8 strips 1½" × 13".
- Cut 2 strips 2⅜" × width of fabric; then cut into 28 squares 2⅜" × 2⅜".
- Cut 3 strips 1⅞" × width of fabric; then cut into 48 squares 1⅞" × 1⅞".
- Cut 2 strips 2" × width of fabric; then cut into 48 rectangles 2" × 1¼".
- Cut 4 squares 3½" × 3½" for the corners.

Light red, yellow, green, and blue

- Cut 1 strip 1½" × 13" from each (4 total).

- Cut 2 squares 4¼" × 4¼" from each (8 total).

Dark red, yellow, green, and blue

- Cut 1 strip 3¼" × width of fabric from each; then cut into 3 squares 3¼" × 3¼" (12 total).

SEW

1. Using the 4¼" × 4¼" light-colored squares and the 2⅜" × 2⅜" background squares, sew 28 large Flying Geese that measure 2" × 3½" unfinished. (Refer to Four-at-a-Time Flying Geese, page 120.) You will have some extra pieces.

2. Using the 3¼" × 3¼" dark-colored squares and the 1⅞" × 1⅞" background squares, sew 48 small Flying Geese. (Refer to Four-at-a-Time Flying Geese, page 120.)

3. Trim the small Flying Geese to 1¼" × 2".

TIP: For tiny geese, it is more accurate to make them larger and trim them to size.

4. Working with a single color family at a time, sew the 1¼" × 2" background rectangles to the small Flying Geese, alternating sides. Sew 2 pieced units to a large Flying Geese unit as shown to create a block. Repeat this step to make a total of 24 blocks.

Flying Geese blocks—make 24.

5. Sew 2 background strips to either side of a color strip to create 4 strip sets. Press the seams open.

6. Working with a single color family at a time, sew together 6 Flying Geese blocks, the remaining

large Flying Geese unit, and a strip set as shown to create the border strips.

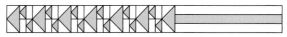

Border 5 assembly

7. Sew the corner squares to each end of the 2 side border strips (for this quilt, the green and yellow borders).

Border 6

FABRIC

Gray: ¼ yard

CUT

Gray

- Cut 2 strips 1½" × 38½".

- Cut 2 strips 1½" × 40½".

Note: If your fabric is not wide enough, you may need to piece the strips so they are long enough.

Border 7

FABRIC

Background: ¼ yard

Dark gray: ¼ yard

CUT

Background

- Cut 5 strips 1½" × 25".

- Cut 2 squares 1½" × 1½" for corners.

Dark gray

- Cut 5 strips 1½" × 25".

- Cut 2 squares 1½" × 1½" for corners.

SEW

1. Sew together all the long strips lengthwise, alternating dark and light as shown, to make a strip set. Press the seam allowance away from the background fabric.

2. Cut the strip set every 1½" perpendicular to seams to yield a total of 16 strips. *Figure C*

3. Sew 4 strips end to end to create a 40½" border strip. Repeat this step to make a total of 4 border strips. *Figure D*

4. Sew the dark and light corner squares to each end of 2 border strips, maintaining the pattern. *Figure E*

TIP: Starching the strip set before cutting will help keep it from warping or stretching.

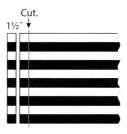

Figure C: Cut 16 from strip set.

Figure D: Border 7 assembly: top and bottom

Figure E: Border 7 assembly: left and right

Border 8

FABRIC

Gray: ¼ yard

CUT

Gray

Note: You will need to piece the strips so they are long enough.

- Cut 5 strips 1½" × width of fabric and sew them together end to end.

- From this continuous strip, cut 2 strips 1½" × 42½" and 2 strips 1½" × 44½".

Border 9

FABRIC

Background: 1⅔ yards

Green, yellow, and blue (4 shades each for a total of 12 fabrics): 1 scrap of each from fat quarters

Red (4 shades): 1 scrap of each from fat quarters

CUT

Background

- Cut 15 strips 1¾" × width of fabric; then cut into 320 squares 1¾" × 1¾".

- Cut 5 strips 1½" × width of fabric; then cut into 40 strips 1½" × 4½".

- Cut 8 strips 1½" × 6½".

- Cut 8 strips 1½" × 44½". (Piece shorter scraps together as needed, or cut 9 width-of-fabric strips and sew together into a single continuous piece.)

Green, yellow, and blue (12 fabrics)

- Cut 12 squares 2½" × 2½" from each fabric (144 total).

Red (4 fabrics)

- Cut 4 squares 2½" × 2½" from each fabric (16 total).

SEW

1. Place 2 background squares on top of a solid square and stitch diagonally across each background square as shown. *Note: Flip up the corners of the background squares so you don't stitch over them.* Trim the corners to a ¼" seam allowance and press toward the background. *Figure F*

TIP: Because the squares are so small, I did not need to draw a diagonal stitching line or pin the fabric, which was a huge time saver. You are welcome to do one or both if that works better for you.

2. Sew together a unit in each shade of a color, as shown, to create the X blocks. Press the seam allowances in the direction of the arrows, so they nest together when sewn. Make a total of 40 X blocks. Set aside the 4 red X blocks to use as corner blocks. *Figure G*

TIP: NESTING SEAMS

Nesting the seams will allow them to lie flat and line up more precisely. To do this,

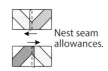
Nest seam allowances.

press the seams to be joined in opposite directions. When you place the pieces right sides together, the seams will butt up against each other or nest, helping them to nestle together.

  Flip corners up, so you don't sew over them.

Figure F:
X block construction

Figure G:
X block assembly—make 40.

Figure H:
Corner block assembly

3. Sew together 9 X blocks and 8 background 1½" × 4½" strips. Press the seams toward the background.

4. Sew the background 44½" strip to the long edges of the border strip. Press the seams toward the background.

5. Repeat Steps 3 and 4 to make a total of 4 border strips.

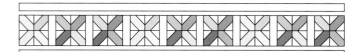

Border 9 assembly

6. To make the corner blocks, sew 1½" × 4½" background strips to the sides of the 4 remaining X blocks. Then sew 1½" × 6½" background strips to the top and bottom. Press the seams toward the background. *Figure H*

7. Sew the corner blocks to each end of the 2 side border strips.

Border 10

FABRIC

Aqua: ⅜ yard

Gray: ⅜ yard

CUT

Aqua

- Cut 4 strips 3" × 36½".

Gray

- Cut 4 strips 3" × 10½".

- Cut 4 strips 3" × 13".

SEW

1. Sew the 10½" strips to either end of a center 36½" strip. Press the seams open. Repeat to make a total of 2.

2. Sew the 13" strips to either end of a center 36½" strip. Press the seams open. Repeat to make a total of 2.

QUILT ASSEMBLY

If you did not add the borders as you made them, assemble the quilt top now.

LAST BORDER SEWN TO TOP	YOUR QUILT SHOULD MEASURE (including seam allowance)
Center medallion	21½" × 21½"
Border 1	25½" × 25½"
Border 2	27½" × 27½"
Border 3	29½" × 29½"
Border 4	32½" × 32½"
Border 5	38½" × 38½"
Border 6	40½" × 40½"
Border 7	42½" × 42½"
Border 8	44½" × 44½"
Border 9	56½" × 56½"
Border 10	61½" × 61½"

1. Assemble the quilt by adding the borders to the center medallion: Sew the shorter Border 1 strips to the top and bottom of the center medallion. Then sew the longer Border 1 strips to the left and right sides. Because the quilt is a square, you will always sew the shorter borders on first, but it is your preference whether you start with the top and bottom or the sides. However, your choice will affect the look of Borders 2 and 3.

2. Continue sewing the top and bottom first and then the sides for each consecutive border. Refer to the quilt assembly diagram (below) to orient the pieced borders correctly. Press the seams as you go.

TIP: To reduce bulk, press the seam allowances toward the border that has the fewest seams.

QUILTING AND FINISHING

Layer the backing, batting, and quilt top. Baste.

Quilt and bind using your preferred methods.

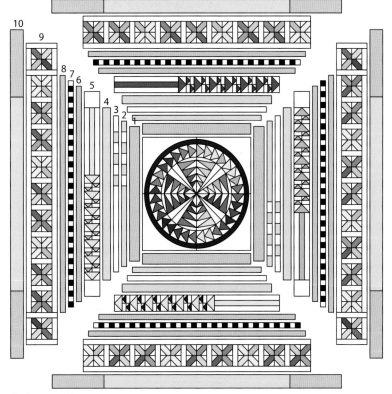

Quilt assembly

WATCH THE
BIRDIE

By Kerry Green

Medallion quilts often have a lot of angular straight-line shapes. I wanted to see how I could add circles and a picture element while still retaining a medallion border style. Light, bright, and made of simple repeated shapes, this design radiates from the center with graphic-style birds flying around flowers and leaves. The outer borders expand the birds' environment to a Scandinavian-style forest with abstract Flying Geese soaring over the summer skyline.

—Kerry

ALL MATERIALS NEEDED FOR QUILT

Cream: 2½ yards for background

Pink: a variety to total 1 yard for birds, flower centers, corner squares, and Flying Geese

Green: a variety to total 1 yard for leaves and trees

Orange: a variety to total ½ yard for leaves and Flying Geese

Yellow: a variety to total 1 yard for flowers, second border strips, Flying Geese, and circles

Tan: a variety to total ¼ yard for trees

White felt: small scraps for appliqué

Batting: 56″ × 56″

Backing: 3¼ yards

Binding: ½ yard

FABRIC, CUTTING, AND CONSTRUCTION (BY BORDER)

Note: Make this completely scrappy or cut enough of each shape from one fabric to make a bird or a leaf all from the same fabric. All seam allowances are ¼″. Press after sewing each seam.

Trace Patterns A, B, and C (pullout page P2) onto template plastic and cut them out to make Templates A, B, and C.

Kerry's Medallion Tip

Medallion designs need a great center, but don't forget that the eye needs continued interest as it works its way outward on a quilt. As much time needs to go into designing the borders as goes into planning the middle. A good way to do this is to get your quilt to tell a story so that the center links to the border and then to the next border and so on. This will also give the finished design cohesion, rather than having a series of separate elements sewn together.

Center Medallion

FABRIC

Cream: ½ yard for background

Pink: scraps at least 4″ × 4″ or ¼ yard

CUT

Cream

- Cut 2 strips 4½″ × width of fabric; subcut 12 of Template A for quarter-circle units.

- Cut 1 strip 4½″ × width of fabric; subcut 4 rectangles 1″ × 4½″ and 4 rectangles 4″ × 4½″.

Pink

- Cut 12 of Template B for quarter-circle units (birds).

SEW

1. Refer to Piecing Curves (page 117) to sew a background A and a pink B to make a quarter-circle unit. Repeat to make a total of 3 quarter-circle units.

2. Sew together 2 quarter-circle units as shown to make a semicircle. Press the seam open.

3. Sew a 1″ × 4½″ background rectangle and a 4″ × 4½″ background rectangle to opposite sides of the remaining quarter-circle unit as shown.

4. Sew the units from Steps 2 and 3 together as shown to make a bird block. *Figure A*

5. Repeat Steps 1–3 to make a total of 4 bird blocks.

6. Sew the 4 bird blocks together as shown in the quilt assembly diagram (page 28), rotating each block by 90°. *Figure B*

Figure A: Bird block

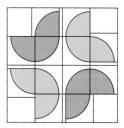

Figure B: Center medallion

Border 1

FABRIC

Cream: 1⅛ yards for background

Green: scraps, each at least 4″ × 4″ or ⅜ yard

Orange: scraps, each at least 4″ × 4″ or ⅛ yard

Pink: 4 small scraps, each at least 3″ × 3″

Yellow: scraps, each at least 4″ × 4″ or ¼ yard

CUT

Cream

- Cut 6 strips 4½″ × width of fabric; then cut 44 of Template A for quarter-circle units.

- Cut 1 strip 4½″ × width of fabric; then cut 32 rectangles ¾″ × 4½″ for leaf backgrounds.

- Cut 1 strip 2½″ × width of fabric; then cut 4 squares 2½″ × 2½″ and 4 rectangles 2½″ × 4½″ for flower backgrounds.

Green

- Cut 24 of Template B for leaves.

Orange

- Cut 8 of Template B for leaves.

Pink

- Cut 4 squares 2½″ × 2½″ for flower centers.

Yellow

- Cut 12 of Template B for flower petals.

SEW

Refer to Piecing Curves (page 117) to make a total of 24 green, 8 orange, and 12 yellow quarter-circle units from Templates A and B.

Figure C: Left-pointing leaf

Leaves

1. Sew a background ¾″ × 4½″ rectangle to the left side of 2 matching green quarter-circle units as shown. Rotate a unit so the added rectangles are opposite each other. Pin to match the quarter-circle seams and sew together as shown. Trim the excess background fabric from each quarter-circle unit to make a leaf unit 4½″ × 8½″ unfinished. *Figure C*

2. Repeat Step 1, but this time sew a ¾″ × 4½″ rectangle to the *right* sides. *Figure D*

3. Repeat Steps 1 and 2 using the green and orange quarter-circles to make a total of 12 left-pointing and 12 right-pointing leaves.

4. Sew a left-pointing leaf to a right-pointing leaf as shown. Repeat this step to make a total of 8 leaf pair blocks. *Figure E*

Figure D: Right-pointing leaf

Figure E: Leaf pair block— make 8.

Flowers

1. Sew a background square to a pink square as shown. Then sew a 2½″ × 4½″ background rectangle to the unit as shown. Repeat to make a total of 4 flower centers.

2. Sew 2 matching yellow quarter-circle units together to make a semicircle.

3. Sew a flower center unit to a side of a yellow quarter-circle. Repeat this step to make 2 and 2 reversed. *Figure F*

Figure F: Flower block— make 2 and 2 reversed.

Assembly

1. Sew 2 leaf pair blocks together as shown. Repeat to make a total of 4 border strips. *Figure G*

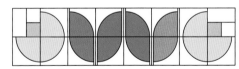

Figure G: Border 1 top and bottom

2. Sew a flower block to each end of 2 of the leaf borders. *Figure H*

Figure H: Border 1 sides

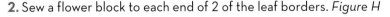

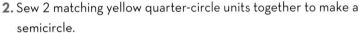
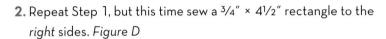

Border 2

FABRIC

Yellow: 1/3 yard

Pink: 2 scraps, each at least 3" × 3"

Green: 2 scraps, each at least 3" × 3"

CUT

Yellow: Cut 4 strips 2½" × 32½".

Pink: Cut 2 corner squares 2½" × 2½".

Green: Cut 2 corner squares 2½" × 2½".

SEW

Sew a pink and a green square to each end of 2 yellow border strips.

Border 3

FABRIC

Cream: 1 yard for background

Pink, orange, and yellow: scraps, each at least 4" × 7", for Flying Geese, and 4 yellow scraps for suns, each at least 6" × 6", to total ¾ yard

Green and tan: scraps, each at least 5½" × 7", for trees to total ⅜ yard

CUT

Cream

- Cut 5 strips 3½" × width of fabric; then cut 48 squares 3½" × 3½" for Flying Geese.

- Cut 2 strips 6½" × width of fabric; then cut 20 of Template C for tree backgrounds.

- Cut 4 squares 6½" × 6½" for corner blocks.

Pink, orange, and yellow

- Cut a total of 24 rectangles 3½" × 6½" for Flying Geese.

Yellow only

- Cut 4 circles 5½" in diameter, using a compass or purchased circle template with scissors, a rotary circle cutter, or a die cutter.

Green and tan

- Cut 18 of Template C for trees.

SEW

1. Refer to One-at-a-Time Flying Geese (page 118) to make a total of 24 Flying Geese, using the 3½" × 3½" background squares and the 3½" × 6½" colored rectangles.

2. Sew 12 Flying Geese together as shown to make a border strip. Repeat to make a second Flying Geese border strip.

Border 3: Flying Geese—make 2.

3. If desired, mark the seam intersection points on the wrong side of the Template C pieces. Starting and ending with a background triangle, sew 11 background and 9 green/tan triangles together as shown. Repeat this step to make a second tree border strip.

Border 3: Trees

4. Square up the short ends of each tree border strip to fit the longer Border 2 strips.

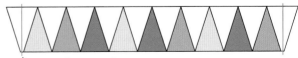

Trim ¼" from triangle.

5. Use your favorite method to appliqué a yellow circle centered on the 6½" × 6½" background square. Repeat this step to make a total of 4 corner blocks. *Note: For raw-edge fusible appliqué, trim ¼" away around the entire circle.*

TIP: To easily turn under the edge of appliqué motifs, try this technique: Tear a square of aluminum foil a little bigger than the diameter of the circle. Place the fabric circle right side down on the dull side of the foil. Place the template on the fabric so it is inside the pencil outline. Fold the foil and fabric tightly in toward the center of the circle, smoothing the edges as you go. Flip over and press the foil circle with a hot dry iron. Allow to cool. Open out and remove the template.

6. Sew a corner block to each end of the 2 tree borders.

Border 3: Trees—make 2.

QUILTING AND FINISHING

1. To make the birds' eyes, cut out 4 small circles from the white felt. Appliqué by hand or machine.

2. Layer the backing, batting, and quilt top. Baste.

3. Cut 6 strips 2¼" × width of fabric for double-fold binding.

4. Quilt and bind using your preferred methods.

QUILT ASSEMBLY

If you did not add the borders as you made them, assemble the quilt top now.

1. Sew the shorter Border 1 strips to the top and bottom of the center medallion. Press.

2. Sew the longer Border 1 strips to the sides of the center medallion. Press.

3. Repeat Steps 1 and 2 to add the remaining borders to the quilt top.

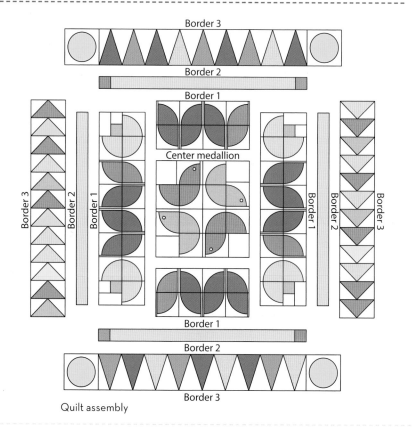

Quilt assembly

DROP OF
GOLDEN SUN

By Karen Anderson-Abraham

This quilt was such fun to create! I love how it allows the quilter to combine improv design, my personal first love in quilting, with some more precise and measured sewing techniques in the wonky stars and the clean overall construction of the quilt itself. I really enjoy the whimsy of the stars contrasted with the super clean, modern minimalism of the rest of the design.

—Karen

ALL MATERIALS NEEDED FOR QUILT

Note: Specific fabric names/colors are included, but feel free to select different fabrics/colors.

Dark green (Kona Everglade) solid: 4½ yards for background

Light gray (Kona Ash) solid: 1¼ yard for borders

Variety of coordinating fabrics: ½–¾ yard for wonky stars

Variety of coordinating color fabric scraps (yellow, teals, blues, grays, lilacs, pinks, white): Use remaining fabric from wonky star blocks and small scraps from stash for center medallion and improv border bits

Batting: 68″ × 68″

Backing: 4 yards

Binding: ½ yard

FABRIC, CUTTING, AND CONSTRUCTION (BY BORDER)

Note: All seam allowances are ¼″.

NOTE: Make all the smaller (4″ and 7″) wonky star blocks first. Then use any resulting small scraps for the improv center medallion star and the improv bits in the border strips.

Use a design wall to help with color and placement when making the wonky stars, placing the star points, and adding the improv bits in the borders.

When all the improvisational piecing is completed, use the design wall again to achieve balance when cutting and laying out borders. Take photographs of the different arrangements and then compare them side by side to make final placement decisions.

Wonky Stars

FABRIC

Dark green: 1/2 yard

Various scraps: approximately 2"–4" each

CUT

Dark green

- *For small star blocks:* Cut 2 strips 1¾" × width of fabric; then subcut 32 squares 1¾" × 1¾" for corner squares and star point backgrounds.

- *For large star blocks:* Cut 2 strips 2¾" × width of fabric; then subcut 16 squares 2¾" × 2¾" for corner squares and star point backgrounds.

Various scraps

- Cut 4 squares 1¾" × 1¾" for small star block centers.

- Cut 2 squares each 2¾" × 2¾" from 8 different fabrics (16 total) for small star points.

- Cut 2 squares 2¾" × 2¾" for large star block centers.

- Cut 1 square 3¾" × 3¾" from 8 different fabrics (8 total) for large star points.

SEW

1. Cut all the star point squares in half diagonally, using a rotary cutter and a ruler.

2. Place a small star point triangle on top of a small 1¾" × 1¾" star point background square, right sides together, as shown. The triangle can be placed at various angles, but fold it down to make sure it will cover the entire bottom right corner of the background square when it is sewn.

3. Sew the triangle to the background square along the long side. Trim the seam allowances to ¼". Press the seam allowances away from background fabric. *Figure A*

TIP: I cut my star point squares 1" larger than the star point background squares to give myself more options for placement, giving the star points varied proportions. This makes it easier to cover the bottom corners without having to line up the star point triangle "just so."

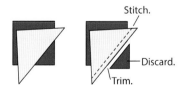

Figure A: Right-side star point

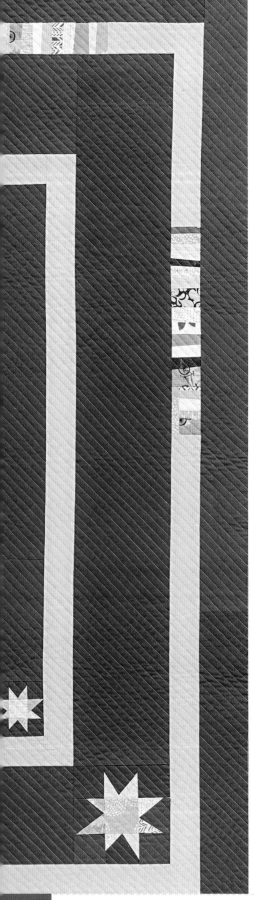

4. Repeat Steps 2 and 3 on the left side of the square. *Figures B & C*

TIP: I lay out all 8 of my triangles for a set of 4 star points first. If you wish to be extra efficient with your time and thread, you can lay out all the squares / star points for all 6 wonky star blocks and chain piece all the star points.

5. Turn over the square and trim to 1¾″ × 1¾″ unfinished. *Figure D*

6. Repeat Steps 2–5 to make a total of 16 small star point squares 1¾″ × 1¾″ and 8 large star point squares 2¾″ × 2¾″.

7. Arrange 4 small star point squares, 4 small background squares, and a small center square on a design wall in 3 rows of 3 to form the wonky star.

8. Sew the units into 3 rows. Press so that seams will nest easily.

9. Sew the rows together, pinning at the seam intersections. Press seams toward the center row. *Figure E*

10. Square the block to 4″ × 4″ unfinished, making sure to trim parallel to the block and row seams. *Figure F*

11. Repeat Steps 7–10 to make a total of 4 small wonky star blocks 4″ × 4″ and 2 large wonky star blocks 7″ × 7″.

Figure B: Left-side star point

Figure C: Star point square ready to be squared up

Figure D: Trim star point square.

Figure E: Sew rows together.

Trim parallel to seam lines.

Figure F: Cutting wonky star block to desired size

Center Medallion

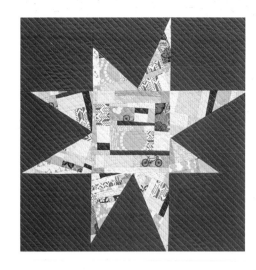

FABRIC

Dark green: 1/2 yard

Various scraps: approximately 1½"–5"

CUT

Dark green: Cut 8 squares 8¾" × 8¾"

SEW

1. Begin "building" the center block by sewing together 2 small pieces at least 1½" × 1½". One can be pieced and then sewn to the original starting piece. *Figure G*

2. Continue adding more pieces and sewing them together as you go, using your design wall for reference. Smaller pieces will give a more energetic look, while larger pieces will give a subtler, calmer feel.

3. Square up the center block to 8¾" × 8¾". *Figure H*

> **TIP:** For a block with many wonky seams, pressing seams to the side is faster than pressing seams open. For a block that lies flat, trim the edges of both pieces to be sewn with a rotary cutter and ruler before sewing. Keep the outer pieces added to the center square larger to make it easier to add the star points.

4. Repeat Steps 1 and 2 to make 4 improv blocks 9¾" × 9¾". Keep the more interesting and complex piecing toward the center of the squares. Again, use larger pieces around the edges of the squares.

5. Cut each 9¾" × 9¾" improv block in half diagonally once to make 8 improv half-square triangles.

6. Refer to Wonky Stars, Sew (page 31) to make 4 star point blocks with the 8 improv half-square triangles and 4 background squares. Then assemble the center star medallion with the improv-pieced center square, star point blocks, and 4 background squares.

7. Trim the center medallion to 25" × 25" unfinished.

> **NOTE:** Use a hot iron with steam to make the star points in each block lie flat where there are many seams.

Figure G: Beginning piecing for center improv square

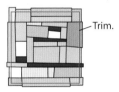

Figure H: Finished center block for center medallion star

> **NOTE:** Be as intricate as you like with multiple seams—as long as you are careful to press well (I like steam) after *each seam*!

Border 1

FABRIC

Light gray: 1/3 yard

Various scraps: 1"–3" wide × 8"–9" long

CUT

Light gray: Cut 2 or 3 strips 2½" × width of fabric.

> **NOTE:** This design calls for improv bits in the borders. How many and where you add them will be totally up to you. These additions will determine how much of the light gray border fabric you'll need for each border strip. You will need 4 border strips: 2 strips 2½" × 25" and 2 strips 2½" × 29".

Improv bits: Cut 8"- to 9"-long strips of varying widths (between 1" and 3") of as many coordinating fabrics as you wish. Cut strips in different widths and at slight angles, so that they are smaller on one side and bigger on the other.

Improv bits strip cutting

> **NOTE:** Adjust this basic technique and the measurements according to how many of the improv bits you want in the borders.

SEW

Making the Improv Bits

1. Sew together the improv strips, alternating the narrow and wide ends and varying the widths and fabrics used.

2. Continue piecing until the strip is about 30" long. Press.

3. Trim the improv-bits strip into 3 strips 2½" wide.

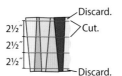

Sew together strips, and cut down to 2½"-wide strips.

4. Cut improv strips into smaller bits or leave long. Square up the ends.

Making the Border Strips

1. Sew the improv bits where desired to the 2½"-wide gray strips along the short sides.

2. Trim as needed to make 2 border strips 2½" × 25" and 2 border strips 2½" × 29".

Sewing the Border Strips to the Quilt

1. Sew the 2½" × 25" strips to the top and bottom of the center medallion. Press the seam allowances toward the borders.

2. Sew the 2½" × 29" strips to the right and left sides. Press the seam allowances toward the borders.

Border 2

FABRIC

Dark green: 1/2 yard

CUT

Dark green

- Cut 2 strips 4″ × 29″.
- Cut 2 strips 4″ × 32½″.

SEW

Making the Border Strips

1. Use the design wall to decide which small wonky star blocks to place at the top left and bottom right corners.

2. Sew a star to an end of each 4″ × 32½″ strip. Press toward the border strip.

Sewing the Border Strips to the Quilt

1. Sew the 4″ × 29″ background strip to the top and bottom of the quilt top.

2. Press the seam allowances toward the Border 2 strips.

3. Sew the star border strips to the sides of the quilt top. The seams should nest easily.

Border 3

FABRIC

Light gray: 1/3 yard

Various scraps or leftover improv bits from Border 1 (page 34)

CUT

Light gray: Cut 3 or 4 strips 2½″ × width of fabric. (Amount varies depending on how much improv piecing will be added to each border. You need 2 border strips 2½″ × 36″ and 2 border strips 2½″ × 40″.)

SEW

Making the Improv Bits

1. Use any remaining improv bits strips from Border 1 or repeat Steps 1–4 in Border 1, Making the Improv Bits (page 34), to piece additional sections.

Making the Border Strips

1. Cut the improv bits as desired and sew the short ends to the background 2½″ × width of fabric strips as desired.

2. Trim down to make 2 border strips 2½″ × 36″ and 2 border strips 2½″ × 40″.

Sewing the Border Strips to the Quilt

1. Sew the shorter border strips to the top and bottom of the quilt top. Press.

2. Sew the longer border strips to the sides of the quilt top. Press.

> **NOTE:** If the border strip has a lot of improv bits in it, pressing it away from itself can be tricky (because of the star points in Border 2)! Two words: steam and hot. Be sure to press, not iron.

Border 4

FABRIC

Dark green: 1 yard

CUT

Dark green: Cut 5 strips 7″ × width of fabric.

SEW

Making the Border Strips

1. Sew the 5 width-of-fabric strips into a single long piece.

2. Subcut into 2 strips 7″ × 40″ and 2 strips 7″ × 46½″.

3. Use the design wall to decide which large wonky star block to place at the top left and bottom right corners.

4. Sew a star to an end of each 7″ × 46½″ strip. Press toward the border strip.

Sewing the Border Strips to the Quilt

Follow the steps in Border 2, Sewing the Border Strips to the Quilt (page 35) to add the top and bottom and then the side borders.

Border 5

FABRIC

Light gray: 3/8 yard

Various scraps or leftover improv pieces from Border 1 (page 34)

CUT

Light gray: Cut 4 or 5 strips 2½″ × width of fabric. (Amount varies depending on improv piecing. You need 2 strips 2½″ × 53″ and 2 strips 2½″ × 57″.)

SEW

Making the Border Strips

1. Follow the steps in Border 3 (page 35) to make and sew improv-bits sections to the 2½″ strips.

2. Sew additional 2½″ × width of fabric strips to the improv-bits borders and trim as needed to make 2 strips that are 2½″ × 53″ and 2 strips that are 2½″ × 57″.

Sewing the Border Strips to the Quilt

Follow the steps in Border 3, Sewing the Border Strips to the Quilt (page 35) to add the top and bottom and then the side borders.

Border 6

FABRIC

Dark green: 1¾ yards, or ¾ yard if pieced

CUT

Dark green

- Cut 2 strips 4″ × 57″ on the lengthwise grain (or piece together shorter strips as needed).

- Cut 2 strips 4″ × 60½″ on the lengthwise grain (or piece together shorter strips as needed).

SEW

Making the Border Strips

Follow the steps in Border 1 to sew the remaining 2 small wonky star blocks to the 60½″ dark green background strips.

Sewing the Border Strips to the Quilt

Follow the steps in Border 2, Sewing the Border Strips to the Quilt (page 35) to add the top and bottom and then the side borders.

QUILT ASSEMBLY

The following is a quick reference guide to keep you on track as you assemble your quilt.

LAST BORDER SEWN TO TOP	YOUR QUILT SHOULD MEASURE (including seam allowance)
Center medallion	25" × 25"
Border 1	29" × 29"
Border 2	36" × 36"
Border 3	40" × 40"
Border 4	53" × 53"
Border 5	57" × 57"
Border 6	64" × 64"

QUILTING AND FINISHING

Layer the backing, batting, and quilt top. Baste.

Quilt and bind using your preferred methods.

TIP: Any extra star blocks can be pieced into the quilt backing.

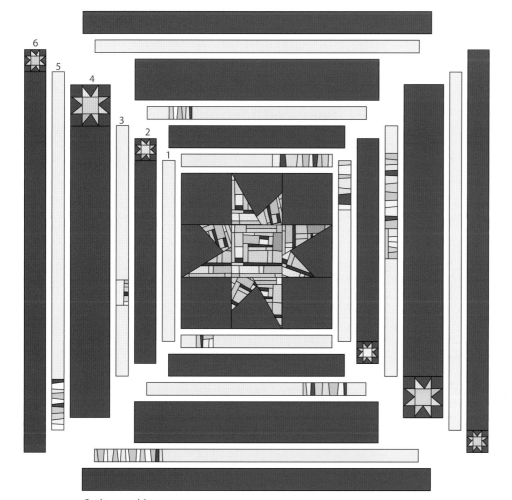

Quilt assembly

ALLIANCE
MEDALLION

By Alexia Marcelle Abegg

When designing quilts, I am often inspired by a particular memory of a time and place, and Alliance Medallion is no different. My father was born and raised in Alliance, a small railroad town in western Nebraska—a part of Nebraska that feels like the beginning of the West, tumbleweeds and all. The town is a stone's throw from Colorado and Wyoming. The idea for this quilt sprang from images of chambray and denim work shirts of my grandfather's generation of railroad engineers and farmers, and of denim quilts made from old, worn work jeans.

With those work shirt images in mind, I chose a variety of chambrays and indigo shot cottons, along with a Liberty of London print for the blue sections. For the pink and red, I used a print by Melody Miller and some more Liberty of London prints.

Last, for the gray and off-white sections, I selected a variety of shot cottons, Japanese prints, and a graphic printed cotton linen by Ellen Luckett Baker. As an alternate variation, this quilt would be fun to make just from the scrap bin, using dark fabrics for the blue sections and light fabrics for the gray/off-white sections.

For the piecing, I started with a Log Cabin center star. The Log Cabin block always evokes a sense of history to me, and it was the first block that came to mind when I began designing this quilt. With fairly straightforward borders, this quilt comes together quite quickly. Finishing at a throw size, this medallion quilt is designed to be loved and used often, just like Grandpa's favorite work shirt.

—Alexia

ALL MATERIALS NEEDED FOR QUILT

Light gray and/or off-white prints: a variety to total 2 yards

Red and/or pink prints: a total of 1/2 yard

Chambray and/or blue prints: a total of 3 yards

Binding: 1/2 yard

Backing: 3 1/2 yards or 1 5/8 yards 60"-wide lightweight chambray (If longarm quilting, you may need to piece a wider backing.)

Batting: 60" × 60" (If longarm quilting, you may need wider batting.)

FABRIC, CUTTING, AND CONSTRUCTION (BY BORDER)

Note: All seam allowances are 1/4". Press after each seam.

Medallion Center

Light gray and/or off-white prints: a variety to total ⅝ yard for center Log Cabin blocks, star background, and corner blocks (Star background requires 1 fat quarter if using only 1 fabric.)

Red and/or pink print: 5″ × 5″ piece for Log Cabin centers

Chambrays and/or blue prints: a variety to total ½ yard for center Log Cabin blocks and star points

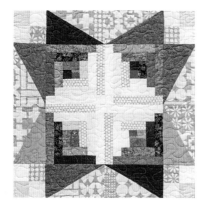

CUT

Light gray and/or off-white

- *For Log Cabin blocks:* Cut 4 strips each of the following sizes:

1½″ × 7½″	1½″ × 4½″
1½″ × 6½″	1½″ × 3½″
1½″ × 5½″	1½″ × 2½″

- *For star background:* Cut 8 rectangles 5″ × 8″; then cut each diagonally as shown into 2 half-rectangle triangles for star background. Discard 4. (If using a fabric with no right or wrong side, only cut 4 rectangles to start.)

Cut 8 half-rectangle triangles (4 and 4 reversed).

- *For corner blocks:* Cut 16 squares 2½″ × 2½″.

Red and/or pink print

- Cut 4 squares 1½″ × 1½″ for Log Cabin centers.

Chambray and/or blue print

- *For Log Cabin blocks:* Cut 4 strips each of the following sizes:

1½″ × 6½″	1½″ × 3½″
1½″ × 5½″	1½″ × 2½″
1½″ × 4½″	

Cut 4 squares 1½″ × 1½″.

- *For star points:* Cut 4 rectangles 5″ × 8″; then cut each diagonally into 2 half-rectangle triangles for the star points. (If using a fabric with definite right and wrong sides, follow cutting instructions for background triangles to start with 8 rectangles.)

SEW

Log Cabin Blocks

1. Sew the red and blue squares together. Press the seam toward the blue square.

2. Sew the blue 1½″ × 2½″ strip to the Log Cabin center. Press the seam toward the most recently sewn strip.

3. Sew the off-white 1½″ × 2½″ strip to the unit as shown. Proceed with the block assembly as shown, pressing seams toward the most recently sewn strip as you go.

4. Repeat Steps 1–3 to complete a total of 4 Log Cabin blocks.

5. Sew together the 4 center Log Cabin blocks to complete the star center as shown in the medallion center assembly diagram. *Figure F*

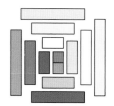

Log Cabin block assembly

Star Points

1. Make the star point units by sewing a blue half-rectangle triangle to a gray/off-white half-rectangle triangle as shown, making sure to offset the corners to allow for the ¼″ seam allowance. Since the long, skinny points can be tricky to line up correctly, this block is designed to be oversized. Press the seams open and trim as needed to 4½″ × 7½″ unfinished, making sure to keep the diagonal seam centered. Repeat to make a total of 4 and 4 reversed. *Figures A–D*

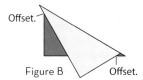

Figure A   Figure B

Figure C: Make 4.   Figure D: Make 4 reversed.

TIP: When you are using solid-colored fabrics with no right or wrong side, it is easy to get half-triangle units mixed up and sewn the wrong way. Lay out the center star to be sure each star point is sewn correctly.

2. Sew together 2 opposite star point units along the light-colored side. Repeat this step to complete 4 sets of star points. *Figure E*

Figure E: Complete star point set

3. Sew the 4 corner Four-Patch blocks with 4 squares 2½″ × 2½″ as shown. *Figure F*

Medallion Center Assembly

1. Sew a star point set to either side of the Log Cabin star center, matching the blue sides as shown. Press the seams toward the Log Cabin center.

2. Sew a Four-Patch block to each end of a star point set. Press the seams toward the four-patches. Repeat this step with the remaining star point set and four-patches.

3. Sew a star point/four-patch unit to each of the 2 remaining edges of the Log Cabin center. Press the seams toward the Log Cabin center. *Figure F*

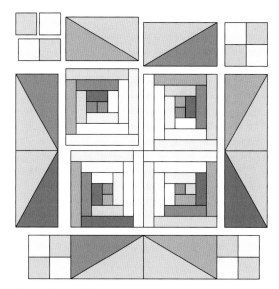

Figure F: Medallion center assembly

Border 1

FABRIC

Light gray and/or off-white print: a variety to total ⅝ yard for half-rectangle triangles

Red and/or pink print: 1 fat quarter for corner squares

Chambray and/or blue print: a variety to total ⅝ yard for half-rectangle triangles

CUT

Light gray and/or off-white print: Cut 22 rectangles 3″ × 9″; then cut each in half diagonally for 2 half-rectangle triangles.

Red and/or pink print: Cut 4 squares 7½″ × 7½″ for corner squares.

Chambray and/or blue print: Cut 22 rectangles 3″ × 9″; then cut each in half diagonally for 2 half-rectangle triangles.

SEW

1. Sew a gray/off-white half-rectangle triangle to a blue half-rectangle triangle as shown and press the seams open. Trim as needed to 2½″ × 7½″ unfinished, making sure to keep the diagonal seam centered. Repeat this step to complete 44 half-rectangle triangle (HRT) units. *Figure G*

2. Sew together 11 HRT units as shown. Press all the seams in the same direction. Repeat this step to complete 4 Border 1 sections. *Figure H*

3. Sew a red/pink square to each end of a border section. Repeat with 1 of the 3 remaining border sections. Press the seams open.

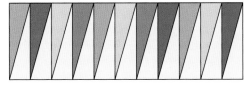

Figure G: Half-rectangle triangle unit assembly

Figure H: Make 4.

Border 2

FABRIC

Red and/or pink print: 8″ × 8″ piece for corner squares

Chambray and/or blue print: ½ yard for border

CUT

Red and/or pink print: Cut 4 squares 3½″ × 3½″ for corner squares.

Chambray and/or blue print: Cut 4 strips 3½″ × 36½″ for border strips.

SEW

Sew 1 red/pink square to each end of a border strip. Repeat with 1 of the 3 remaining border strips. Press the seams open.

Make 2 of each.

Border 3

FABRIC

Light gray and/or off-white print: a variety to total ½ yard for pieced border

Red and/or pink print: 6″ × 6″ piece for corner squares

CUT

Light gray and/or off white print: Cut 84 squares 2½″ × 2½″ for pieced border.

Red and or pink print: Cut 4 squares 2½″ × 2½″ for cornerstones.

SEW

1. Sew 21 gray/off-white 2½″ × 2½″ squares end to end. Press the seams in the same direction.

2. Repeat Step 1 to complete 4 border strips.

Make 4.

3. Sew a red/pink 2½″ × 2½″ square to each end of a border strip. Repeat with 1 of the 3 remaining border strips. Press the seams open.

Make 2.

Border 4

FABRIC

Light gray and/or off-white print: a variety to total ¼ yard for Log Cabin corner blocks

Red and/or pink print: 4″ × 4″ piece for corner squares

Chambray and/or blue print: a variety to total 1¼ yards for Log Cabin corner blocks and pieced rectangle border

CUT

Light gray and/or off-white print

For Log Cabin blocks:

- Cut 4 strips each of the following sizes:

  1½″ × 5½″

  1½″ × 4½″

  1½″ × 3½″

  1½″ × 2½″

Red and/or pink print

- Cut 4 squares 1½″ × 1½″ for Log Cabin centers.

Chambray and/or blue print

For Log Cabin blocks:

- Cut 4 squares 1½″ × 1½″.

- Cut 4 strips each of the following sizes:

  1½″ × 4½″

  1½″ × 3½″

  1½″ × 2½″

- Cut 92 rectangles 2½″ × 5½″ for pieced rectangle borders.

SEW

1. Sew 23 blue rectangles together along the long sides. Press all the seams in the same direction.

2. Repeat Step 1 to complete 4 border strips. *Figure I*

Figure I: Make 4.

3. Repeat Log Cabin Blocks, Steps 1–4 (page 40) with the red squares and blue and light gray 1½"-wide strips to complete 4 Log Cabin blocks. *Figure J*

Figure J: Log Cabin block assembly—make 4.

4. Sew a Log Cabin block to each end of a border section as shown. Repeat with 1 of the 3 remaining border sections. Press the seams open. *Figure K*

Figure K: Make 2.

QUILT ASSEMBLY

Assemble the quilt as shown, adding a border at a time to the center medallion block.

When you sew each border, add the border units without corner blocks first, and then add the border units with the corner blocks. Press the seams out toward the outer edges of the quilt as you go. Take care not to stretch the quilt when assembling.

If your strips are too long, trim down as needed. You may wish to remove the corner blocks/cornerstones first, trim the borders, and then reattach the corner pieces.

QUILTING AND FINISHING

Layer the backing, batting, and quilt top. Baste.

Quilt and bind using your preferred methods.

Quilt assembly

OVIEDO
MEDALLION

By Erica Jackman

The fabrics used in this quilt are from the Clover Sunshine and Sun Print lines designed by Alison Glass for Andover Fabrics.

This was the first project that I designed after moving into a new home in a new city. The process reminded me of starting over and making something from scratch. For that reason, I named it after the name of our street. I wanted the colors to evoke hope and happiness.

—Erica

ALL MATERIALS NEEDED FOR QUILT

Colored prints: a variety totaling 6½ yards

Background: a variety of low-volume prints totaling 3⅞ yards

Backing: 4⅝ yards

Binding: ⅝ yard

Batting: 80″ × 80″

Foundation paper, such as Carol Doak's Foundation Paper or Simple Foundations Translucent Vellum Paper

FABRIC, CUTTING, AND CONSTRUCTION (BY BORDER)

Note: All seam allowances are ¼″. Press all seams open unless otherwise specified.

Copy the patterns (pullout page P2) onto template plastic and cut them out to create Templates A and B.

Center Medallion

FABRIC

Multicolored print: 1 scrap

Teal print: ⅛ yard

Purple print: ¼ yard

Yellow print: ¼ yard

Background: ¼ yard

CUT

Multicolored print

- Cut 1 square 2½″ × 2½″.

Teal print

- Cut 2 rectangles 1½″ × 2½″.
- Cut 2 rectangles 1½″ × 4½″.
- Cut 2 squares 5″ × 5″.

Purple print

- Cut 4 squares 5″ × 5″.

Yellow print

- Cut 1 strip 5″ × width of fabric; then cut into 8 squares 5″ × 5″.

Background

- Cut 1 strip 5″ × width of fabric; then cut into 6 squares 5″ × 5″ and 4 squares 4½″ × 4½″.

SEW

1. Sew a teal rectangle 1½" × 2½" to either side of the 2½" × 2½" multicolored square. Press the seams open, and then sew the 1½" × 4½" teal pieces to the top and bottom of the unit. Press.

2. Refer to Making Half-Square Triangles (page 123) to make a total of 10 half-square triangle (HST) units with the 5" × 5" squares in the following combinations:

   2 teal/yellow

   2 yellow/purple

   4 yellow/background

   2 purple/background

3. Trim each HST unit to 4½" × 4½".

4. Sew the HST units, 4 background 4½" × 4½" squares, and the center square into 5 rows as shown in the center medallion diagram (below). Then sew the rows together to complete the center medallion.

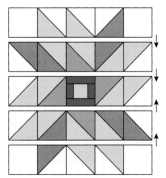

Center medallion

Border 1

Background prints: ⅔ yard total

Pink prints: ⅓ yard total

CUT

Background prints

- Cut 3 strips 3½" × width of fabric; then cut into 24 squares 3½" × 3½".

- Cut 2 strips 3" × width of fabric; then cut into 16 squares 3" × 3".

- Cut 1 strip 5½" × width of fabric; then cut into 4 squares 5½" × 5½".

Pink prints

- Cut 3 strips 3½" × width of fabric; then cut into 24 squares 3½" × 3½".

SEW

1. Pair the 24 pink 3½″ × 3½″ squares with the background 3½″ × 3½″ squares to make a total of 48 HST units (see Making Half-Square Triangles, page 123).

2. Trim the HST units to 3″ × 3″.

3. Refer to the block assembly   diagram: Sew an HST unit to a 3″ × 3″ background square. Sew together 2 HST
Block assembly
units. Then sew the 2 units together. Repeat this step to make a total of 16 pieced blocks.

4. Sew together 4 of the blocks into border strips. Repeat this step to make a total of 4.

Border 1—make 4.

5. Sew a 5½″ × 5½″ background square onto the short sides of 2 border strips.

6. Sew the shorter border strips to the top and bottom of the center medallion. Sew the longer strips to the sides.

TIP: When adding each border strip, backstitching at the beginning and end of the seam keeps the weight of the fabric from pulling on the seam.

Border 2

FABRIC

Blue prints: ½ yard total

Green prints: ½ yard total

Orange print: ⅛ yard

Background: ¼ yard total

CUT

Blue prints: Cut 12 strips 2½″ × at least 18″.

Green prints: Cut 12 strips 2½″ × at least 18″.

Orange print: Cut 8 squares 3″ × 3″ and 4 squares 2½″ × 2½″ for Shoofly corner blocks.

Background print: Cut 8 squares 3″ × 3″ and 16 squares 2½″ × 2½″ for Shoofly corner blocks.

SEW

1. Arrange the 2½″ × 18″ strips into 8 groups of 3 strips: 4 green-blue-green (GBG) and 4 blue-green blue (BGB). Sew into strip sets.

2. Cut 3 units 5½″ × 6½″ from each strip set. Make sure to align the ruler lines with the seams.

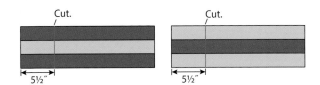

3. Sew together 6 units, alternating BGB with GBG, to make a border strip. Repeat this step to make a total of 4 border strips.

Border 2 assembly

4. Make 4 HST units (see Making Half-Square Triangles, page 123) with the 3″ × 3″ orange squares and 3″ × 3″ background squares. Trim the HSTs to 2½″ × 2½″.

5. Sew 2 HSTs units to either side of a background 2½″ × 2½″ square. Repeat this step to make a total of 2.

6. Sew 2 background 2½″ × 2½″ squares to either side of an orange 2½″ × 2½″ square.

7. Sew the 3 background/orange units together as shown to make a Shoofly block.

Shoofly block

8. Repeat Steps 4–7 to make a total of 4 Shoofly blocks.

9. Sew a Shoofly block to each end of 2 border strips.

10. Sew the shorter border strips to the top and bottom of the quilt top. Sew the longer strips to the sides.

Border 3

FABRIC

Scraps in various colors and background: a total of approximately 1¼ yards

Paper for foundation piecing

CUT

Paper: Cut the foundation paper into 60 squares 3½″ × 3½″.

Scraps: Cut approximately 250 strips between 1¼″ and 2″ wide and between 2½″ and 5½″ long from a variety of prints and background fabric, including scraps from previous borders. *Make sure you have at least 60 strips 5½″ long.*

SEW

1. Place a 5½″-long strip right side up diagonally across the paper foundation. Place a shorter strip on top of it, right sides together, aligning the long edges. Sew and flip the top strip open, making sure that the fabric covers the paper square. Press. Continue adding strips until the entire paper square is covered. Use about 3–5 strips per block.

Strip should go from corner to corner diagonally, making sure that fabric covers both corners.

Finished block

2. Flip over the block and trim to a 3½″ × 3½″ square, using the foundation paper as a guide. Remove the paper.

3. Piece the blocks into 4 border strips: 2 that are 14 blocks long and 2 that are 16 blocks long.

4. Sew the shorter border strips to the top and bottom of the quilt top. Sew the longer strips to the sides.

Border 3

Border 4

FABRIC

Background print: 1/2 yard

Orange print: 1/8 yard

CUT

Background print: Cut 5 strips 2½" × width of fabric.

Orange print: Cut 4 squares 2½" × 2½".

SEW

1. Piece the 5 width-of-fabric strips into a continuous strip.

2. Cut the strip into 4 strips 2½" × 48½".

3. Sew a 2½" × 2½" orange square to each short end of 2 border strips.

4. Sew the shorter border strips to the top and bottom of the quilt top. Sew the longer strips to the sides.

Border 5

FABRIC

Background print: 3/4 yard

Purple prints: 2/3 yard total

Rainbow print: 1/8 yard

CUT

Background prints: Cut 7 strips 3¾" × width of fabric; then cut into 64 squares 3¾" × 3¾".

Purple prints: Cut 32 rectangles 3¾" × 7".

Rainbow print: Cut 4 squares 3¾" × 3¾".

SEW

1. Make Flying Geese units using purple rectangles and background squares (refer to One-at-a-Time Flying Geese, page 118). Make 32 units.

2. Sew together 8 Flying Geese units along the short edges to create a border strip.

3. Repeat Step 2 to make a total of 4 border strips.

4. Sew a rainbow square to each short end of 2 border strips.

5. Sew the shorter border strips to the top and bottom of the quilt top. Sew the longer strips to the sides.

Border 6

FABRIC

Pink print: 2/3 yard

CUT

Pink print: Cut 7 strips 3¼" × width of fabric.

SEW

1. Piece the 7 width-of-fabric strips into a continuous piece.

2. Cut the piece into 2 strips 3¼" × 59" and 2 strips 3¼" × 64½".

Border 7

FABRIC

Pink, orange, yellow, green, teal, blue, and purple prints: ⅛ yard each

Background: 1¼ yards total

CUT

Pink, orange, yellow, green, teal, blue, and purple prints: Cut 8 of Pattern A from teal and 10 of Pattern A from each of the other colors.

Background: Cut 9 strips 4⅝" × width of fabric. Subcut 68 of Pattern B.

SEW

> **NOTE:** Piecing these curves is not difficult, but it does take some practice. Experiment with pinning or not pinning until you find a method that works well for you.

1. Refer to Piecing Curves (page 117) to sew 68 quarter-circle blocks using the A and B pieces.

   TIP: Be careful not to stretch the fabric as you piece these blocks because they will not lie flat. There is a little wiggle room to square up later, so don't worry if they aren't perfect.

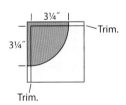

Figure A: Trim block so there is 3¼" from corner to curve.

2. Square up the block so that the quarter-circle sides both measure 3¼" and the overall block is 4½" × 4½" unfinished. *Figure A*

3. Arrange the blocks around the quilt or on your design wall. Arrange 2 rows of 16 blocks and 2 rows of 18 blocks.

4. Sew together 2 border strips of 16 blocks each.

5. Sew together 2 border strips of 18 blocks each.

6. Sew the shorter border strips to the top and bottom of the quilt top. Sew the longer strips to the sides.

QUILT ASSEMBLY

If you did not add the borders as you made them, assemble the quilt top now.

LAST BORDER SEWN TO TOP	YOUR QUILT SHOULD MEASURE (including seam allowance)
Center medallion	20½″ × 20½″
Border 1	30½″ × 30½″
Border 2	42½″ × 42½″
Border 3	48½″ × 48½″
Border 4	52½″ × 52½″
Border 5	59″ × 59″
Border 6	64½″ × 64½″
Border 7	72½″ × 72½″

QUILTING AND FINISHING

Layer the backing, batting, and quilt top. Baste.

Quilt and bind using your preferred methods.

Quilt assembly

JUNE
MEDALLION

By Beth Vassalo

For June Medallion, I started with a very simple center square, surrounded it with fourteen borders—some of which are just strips of different neutral solid and low-volume print fabrics and some that are more intricately pieced—and finished with a scrappy binding. The quilt is designed to be improvisationally pieced to give you the freedom to customize your version. I enjoyed working border by border on this quilt, carefully selecting each fabric, and using a simple design wall to audition each border before sewing it to the quilt. One of my favorite aspects of June Medallion is that each border includes either negative space or randomly sized scrappy pieces, making it especially easy for the borders to be trimmed to fit. You can set aside any concerns about precise cutting and piecing, and instead concentrate on fabric play and design!

—Beth

ALL MATERIALS NEEDED FOR QUILT

Bright print scraps: a variety totaling approximately 1 yard

Dot background: a variety totaling approximately 3¼ yards

Solid background: a variety totaling approximately 1 yard

Binding: assorted scraps totaling ½ yard

Backing: 3½ yards

Batting: 61″ × 61″

FABRIC, CUTTING, AND CONSTRUCTION (BY BORDER)

*Important: Cut, construct, and attach each border as it is made. Do **not** cut background fabric for unpieced borders until you are ready to sew them in place. Measure the quilt top before cutting each border, as sizes may vary due to the improvisational style. Square up each pair of border strips attached before sewing on the next pair.*

Note: All seam allowances are ¼″ unless otherwise stated. However, to add a slight curve or wave to some of the longer unpieced border seams, vary the seam allowance (between ¼″ and ⅝″) within a single seam. For improvisational piecing with small scraps, use a shorter stitch length than normal to make sure short seams won't open up when trimmed to size.

Press seams open.

Center Medallion

FABRIC

Green: a small scrap at least 4″ × 4″

Yellow: a scrap at least 1½″ × 18″

Dot background: a fat eighth or scrap at least 8″ × 8″

CUT

Green: Cut 1 square 3½″ × 3½″ for center.

Yellow: Cut 2 strips 1″ × 3½″ and 2 strips 1″ × 4½″ for sashing.

Dot background: Cut 1 square 8″ × 8″; then cut diagonally twice into 4 quarter-square setting triangles.

SEW

1. Sew the 1″ × 3½″ strips to 2 opposite sides of the green center square. Press.

2. Sew the 1″ × 4½″ strips to the top and bottom. Press.

3. Sew a quarter-square triangle to 2 opposite sides of the center square, centering the square. Press.

4. Sew the remaining quarter-square triangles centered to the top and bottom of the center square. Press. *Note: Be sure the edges of the triangle extend past the edges of the previously sewn triangles.*

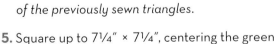

5. Square up to 7¼″ × 7¼″, centering the green square on point.

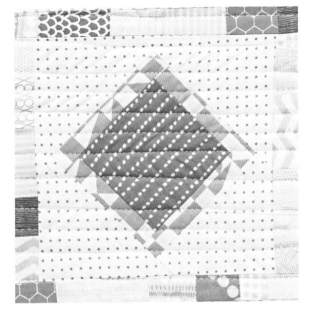

Border 1

FABRIC

Bright print scraps: a variety, each measuring at least 2″ × 2″

SEW

1. Sew together scraps to make 2 strips at least 8½″ long and 2 strips at least 10″ long.

TIP: Piece the scraps together with straight seams (trimming with a rotary cutter as needed) or follow the edge of the scrap for a slightly angled or curved seam.

2. Trim all the strips to 1¼″ wide.

Border 2

FABRIC

Bright print scraps:

1 large scrap each of 2 different fabrics

Dot background: ¼ yard

CUT

Bright print

- Cut 3 rectangles approximately 2″ × 2½″ from each fabric for improv Flying Geese.

Dot background

- Cut 12 squares approximately 2½″ × 2½″. (*Note: Cutting the background squares larger than the height of the geese rectangles makes it easier to make improv Flying Geese, but it uses more fabric. Decide what is best for you.*)

- Cut a strip 2½″ × width of fabric for the border strips. Measure the quilt across the width and cut 2 strips to fit the top and bottom borders. Reserve the rest for the side borders.

SEW

1. Refer to One-at-a-Time Flying Geese (page 118) to make 6 improv Flying Geese with the bright print rectangles and the background squares. To make the geese improv, don't align the outer corner of the squares perfectly with each corner of the rectangle. Place the squares at varying angles as shown, or vary where the top point of the triangle will fall. Trim the excess layers at the corner, but do not square up the Flying Geese units yet. *Figures A–C*

2. Square up the top and bottom edges of each Flying Geese unit so they are parallel. Trim the Flying Geese units to 2½″ wide. Vary the placement of the print triangle within each unit, but make sure to leave at least ¼″ of background fabric on the top and sides, so the points won't be lost in the seam allowance. *Figures D and E*

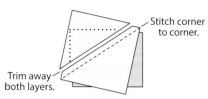

Stitch corner to corner.

Trim away both layers.

Figure A: Angle top square.

Flip and press.

Figure B: Press open.　　　Figure C

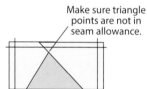

Make sure triangle points are not in seam allowance.

Figure D: Allow for ¼″ seam allowance.

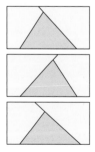
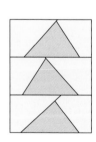

Figure E: Vary triangle placement.　　　Figure F

3. Sew together 3 Flying Geese units of the same color into a column as shown. Repeat with the remaining 3 Flying Geese. *Figure F*

4. Cut the remaining 2½" background strip into 2 equal pieces.

5. Sew the background strips to a short end of each Flying Geese column. Refer to the quilt assembly diagram (page 62) for placement or use your design wall to determine your preferred layout. Measure the length of the quilt top after attaching the top and bottom borders and cut the side border strips to fit.

Border 3

FABRIC

Solid background: ⅛ yard

CUT

Solid background: Cut 2 strips 1¾" × width of fabric; then cut 2 strips 1¾" × 12¾" and 2 strips 1¾" × 15¼".

Border 4

FABRIC

Dot background: ¼ yard

CUT

Dot background: Cut 2 strips 2½" × width of fabric; then cut 2 strips 2½" × 15¼" and 2 strips 2½" × 19¼".

Border 5

FABRIC

Scraps: a variety, each measuring at least 2" × 2".

SEW

1. Repeat the steps for Border 1 (page 55) to make 2 scrappy strips 1¼" × at least 22" and 2 scrappy strips 1¼" × at least 24".

Border 6

FABRIC

Dot background: ¼ yard

CUT

Dot background: Cut 4 strips 1½" × width of fabric; then cut 2 strips 1½" × 20¾" and 2 strips 1½" × 22¾".

Border 7

FABRIC

Solid background: ¼ yard

CUT

Solid background: Cut 4 strips 1¼" × width of fabric; then cut 2 strips 1¼" × 24¾" and 2 strips 1¼" × 24¼".

Border 8

FABRIC

Dot background: ¼ yard

CUT

Dot background: Cut 4 strips 1¼" × width of fabric; then cut 2 strips 1¼" × 24¼" and 2 strips 1¼" × 25¾".

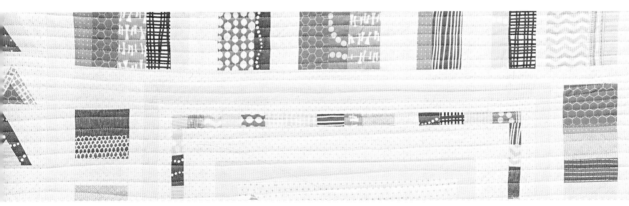

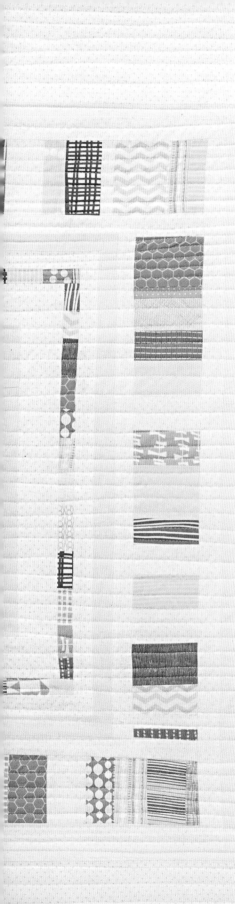

Border 9

FABRIC

Scraps: a variety, each measuring at least 1″ × 3½″

Dot background: ⅛ yard or scraps from previous borders

CUT

Dot background: Cut 1 strip 4″ × width of fabric.

SEW

1. Sew together a group of 2–5 scraps along the long edges. Press.

2. Cut a piece any width from the background strip and sew to an end of the scrappy strip.

3. Repeat Steps 1 and 2 to continue making scrappy/background strips. Sew together to make 2 border strips at least 36″ long for the top and bottom borders and 2 border strips at least 29″ long that begin and end with a 1½″-wide background scrap.

4. Trim all the border strips to 3½″ wide.

Border 10

FABRIC

Dot background: ¼ yard

CUT

Dot background: Cut 4 strips 1¾″ × width of fabric; then cut 2 strips 1¾″ × 31¾″ and 2 strips 1¾″ × 34¼″.

Border 11

FABRIC

Solid background: ⅛ yard

CUT

Solid background: Cut 4 strips 1″ × width of fabric; then cut 2 strips 1″ × 34½″ and 2 strips 1″ × 35¼″.

Border 12

FABRIC

Bright prints: 7 small scraps, each at least 2½" × 3½", and 7 larger scraps, each about 3" × 10"

Dot background: 1⅛ yards

CUT

Bright prints

- Cut 2 corners off each small scrap at varied angles to make 6 improv triangles.

- Cut 2 strips at least 1½" × 5" from each larger scrap (14 total).

Dot background

- Cut 6 strips 5" × width of fabric for border strips.

- Cut 1 strip 5½" × width of fabric; then cut 7 squares 5½" × 5½". Cut each square in half diagonally once for triangle block backgrounds.

SEW

1. Sew a bright print strip 1½" × 5" centered to a side of a triangle. Press. Trim the ends of the strip even with the sides of the triangle as shown. *Figure G*

2. Sew the matching 1½" × 5" strip to the other side of the triangle. Press seams. Trim the ends of the strip even with the sides of the triangle; then trim the sides of the strips at varied angles if desired. *Figure H*

3. Repeat Steps 1 and 2 to make a total of 7 sashed triangles.

4. Sew a background triangle to each side of the sashed triangles, similar to making the improv Flying Geese in Border 2, Step 1 (page 56). Vary the triangle placement so that the sashed triangles have differing amounts of background fabric on each side.

5. Square up the top and bottom edges of each sashed triangle unit so they are parallel.

6. Use a design wall to arrange the sashed triangle units as shown in the quilt assembly diagram (page 62).

Trim even with triangle sides.

Figure G

Trim.

Trim sides at wonky angles.

Figure H

7. Trim the sashed triangle units for the side borders to 5″ wide. Vary the placement of the triangles from left to right and make sure to allow for a ¼″ seam allowance at the top of the triangle. *Figure I*

8. Trim the sashed triangle units for the bottom border to 5″ high. If the units are not tall enough, or to vary the placement of smaller triangles within the border, add background strips to the top or bottom of the unit as needed. *Figures J and K*

9. Sew sashed triangle units into rows or columns following the layout or quilt assembly diagram (page 62). Then sew a 5″ × width of fabric background strip to a short end of each triangle strip as shown in the quilt assembly diagram. *Figures L–N*

10. Cut a 6″-long piece from a width-of-fabric background strip and sew it to the other short end of a side border strip.

11. Sew the remaining background strip from Step 10 to the last remaining background strip for the top border.

Leave at least ¼″ on all sides of triangle.

Figure I: Trim.

Figure J

5″

Figure K

Figure L

Figure M: Side border

Figure N: Bottom border

Border 13

FABRIC

Solid background: ¼ yard

CUT

Solid background: Cut 5 strips 1¼″ × width of fabric.

SEW

Sew strips end to end to make a continuous strip. Cut into 2 strips at least 1¼″ × 44¼″ and 2 strips at least 1¼″ × 45¾″.

Border 14

FABRIC

Dot: ½ yard

CUT

Dot background: Cut 6 strips 2¾″ × width of fabric (or cut 5 and use a scrap).

SEW

Sew strips end to end to make a continuous strip. Cut into 2 strips at least 2¾″ × 45¾″ and 2 strips at least 2¾″ × 50¼″.

QUILT ASSEMBLY

Note: This project works best if you make each border and then attach it to the quilt top before starting the next step.

If you did not add the borders to the quilt as you made them, use the quilt assembly diagram (page 62) as a guide.

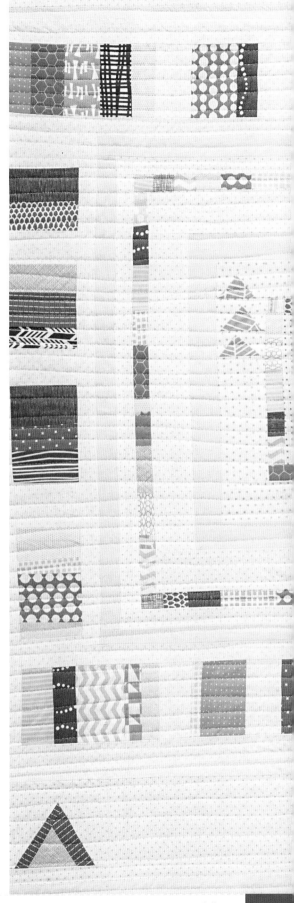

LAST BORDER SEWN TO TOP	YOUR QUILT SHOULD MEASURE (including seam allowance)
Center medallion	7¼″ × 7¼″
Border 1	8¾″ × 8¾″
Border 2	12¾″ × 12¾″
Border 3	15¼″ × 15¼″
Border 4	19¼″ × 19¼″
Border 5	20¾″ × 20¾″
Border 6	22¾″ × 22¾″
Border 7	24¼″ × 24¼″
Border 8	25¾″ × 25¾″
Border 9	31¾″ × 31¾″
Border 10	34¼″ × 34¼″
Border 11	35¼″ × 35¼″
Border 12	44¼″ × 44¼″
Border 13	45¾″ × 45¾″
Border 14	50¼″ × 50¼″

1. Measure the width of the center medallion and trim the shorter Border 1 strips to fit as needed. Sew the border strips to the sides of the quilt. Press.

2. Measure the height of the center medallion, trim the longer Border 1 strips as needed, and sew them to the quilt top. Press.

3. Repeat Steps 1 and 2, measuring the quilt top and trimming borders as needed, until all the borders have been attached. *Note that Border 2 is designed to be sewn to the top and bottom first, and then the sides.*

QUILTING AND FINISHING

Layer the backing, batting, and quilt top. Baste.

Quilt using your preferred methods.

Sew together larger scraps. Cut into long strips 2½" wide. Sew scrappy strips together at the short ends into a continuous piece at least 235" long. Bind using your preferred methods.

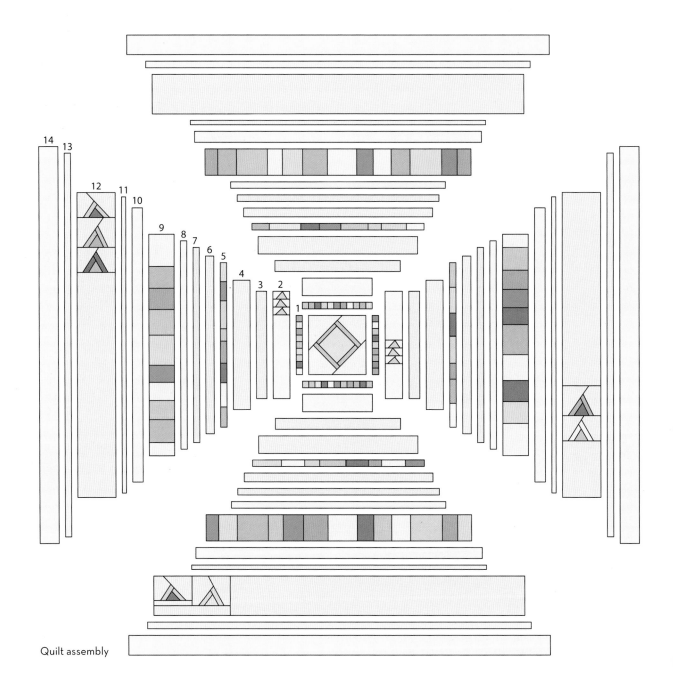

Quilt assembly

WEDDING BOUQUET
MEDALLION

By Rebecca Bryan • Quilted by Danielle Wilkes

I love medallion quilts. So much creative possibility exists from border to border. Only when the last border is sewn is any medallion design truly complete. Even then there's still the binding to consider!

As I was making a classic Pickle Dish quilt, it was natural for me to gravitate toward creating a medallion based on the Pickle Dish motif. I played with the Pickle Dish blocks until I settled on an arrangement that looked like a flower. From that center flower, I built out layers to create a garden. I was thinking about a photograph of a garden in which some flowers are in focus but the background is out of focus and just providing color.

The focal points of this quilt—the Pickle Dish and Orange Peel blocks—can be challenging, so I added easier borders. The easier borders paint the colorful background. I made sure to leave plenty of white space for my favorite quilting motifs. Mine is feathering. What's yours?

—Becca

ALL MATERIALS NEEDED FOR QUILT

Assorted yellow, pink, orange, and green prints: a variety to total 5⅝ yards

White: 5 yards

Lightweight fusible interfacing, 20″ wide: ⅛ yard

Backing: 4 yards

Batting: 78″ × 78″

Binding: ⅝ yard

Foundation paper, such as Carol Doak's Foundation Paper or Simple Foundations Translucent Vellum Paper

FABRIC, CUTTING, AND CONSTRUCTION (BY BORDER)

Note: All seam allowances are ¼″ unless otherwise stated. **Make sure to check that the sizes of completed blocks and borders match the instructions, or your borders may not fit correctly.**

Copy the patterns (pullout page P1) and cut them out to create the Pickle Dish Arc paper foundation and Cutting Templates A, B, C, D, E, and F. You will need 12 copies of the Pickle Dish Arc and 1 copy each of A, B, C, D, E, and F.

Refer to Foundation Paper Piecing (page 124) as needed.

Becca's Medallion Tip

I love making medallions because they allow for such creativity from border to border. They are very much like those "choose your own ending" storybooks I used to read as a child. You have the freedom to nix a border if it isn't going well or fudge it a bit to fit. You can even add your favorite blocks.

Center Medallion

FABRIC

White: 1 yard

Pink prints: a variety to total 3/8 yard

Orange prints: a variety to total 3/8 yard

Yellow prints: a variety to total 1/4 yard

Green prints: a variety to total 1/8 yard

CUT

White

- Cut 8 of Pattern B.

- Cut 2 squares 18 " × 18". Cut in half diagonally once for corner triangles. (Triangles are cut oversized and will be trimmed later.)

Pink prints

- Cut 32 strips 2½" × 5".

Orange prints

- Cut 32 strips 2½" × 5".

Yellow prints

- Cut 32 squares 2³/8" × 2³/8".

Green prints

- Cut 4 of Pattern A.

SEW

1. Make 8 four-patches with the yellow 2³⁄₈″ × 2³⁄₈″ squares as shown. Press the seams to the side.

2. Use the pink and orange 2½″ × 5″ strips to paper piece 8 Pickle Dish Arcs, alternating orange and pink. Trim the seam allowance to ¼″ and remove the paper. *Figure A*

3. Fold piece A in half widthwise and crease to create a centerline. With right sides together, match the centerline on piece A with the center seam in a Pickle Dish Arc. Pin at the centers, match points and in between. Sew. Press the seam toward A. (See Piecing Curves, page 117.)

4. Repeat Step 3 with 3 A pieces and 3 arcs.

5. Sew a four-patch to each end of the 4 remaining Pickle Dish arcs. Press the seams toward the four-patches.

6. Pin an arc with a piece A and an arc with 2 four-patches together at the centerlines. Pin the match points and then pin well in between. Sew. Press the seam toward piece A. Repeat this step with the remaining units to make a total of 4 Pickle Dish units.

7. Mark seam intersection points along the curved edge on the wrong side of the B pieces. Sew a B piece to each side of a Pickle Dish unit to complete the block. Begin and end stitching by backstitching at the seam intersection points, leaving the seam allowances free. Repeat this step to make at total of 4 Pickle Dish blocks.

8. Sew together 2 rows of 2 Pickle Dish blocks. Press the seams open. The medallion should measure 23½″ × 23½″ at this point. *Figure B*

9. To set the center medallion on point, pin a corner setting triangle centered to 2 opposite sides of the unit. Sew, being careful not to stretch the bias edges of the triangles. Press the seams outward. Repeat this step to attach the remaining 2 triangles to the other 2 sides. Square up as needed to 33½″ × 33½″ unfinished. *Figure C*

Figure A: Paper piece 8 arcs.

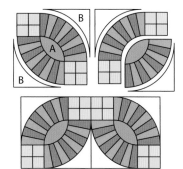

Figure B: Sew together 4 Pickle Dish blocks.

Figure C: Add corner setting triangles.

Border 1

Pink and orange prints: a variety to total 3/8 yard each color

Green prints: a variety to total 1/2 yard

Yellow prints: a variety to total 1/4 yard

White: 3/4 yard

CUT

Pink, orange, green, and yellow prints

- Cut a total of 24 rectangles 3¼" × 6" for Flying Geese. Cut a total of 44 squares 3⅝" × 3⅝" (24 green, 8 pink, 8 orange, and 4 yellow) for half-square triangles.

Pink and orange only

- Cut 16 (8 pink and 8 orange) of Pattern C for the Orange Peel blocks, paying attention to the grainline on the pattern.

White

- Cut 4 strips 3¼" × width of fabric. From each strip, subcut 12 squares 3¼" × 3¼" for Flying Geese. Cut 3 strips 3¼" × width of fabric; subcut 32 of Pattern D for the Orange Peel block backgrounds.

- Cut 4 squares 3⅝" × 3⅝" for half-square triangles.

SEW

Flying Geese Borders

1. Make a total of 24 Flying Geese blocks with the 3¼" × 6" print rectangles and 3¼" × 3¼" white squares (see One-at-a-Time Flying Geese, page 118). Completed Flying Geese should measure 3¼" × 6" unfinished.

> **NOTE:** When possible, I like to piece Flying Geese using the four-at-a-time method (page 120). However, to create the scrappy look in this quilt, I used the one-at-a-time method (page 118) for more variety.

2. Sew together 6 Flying Geese pointing in the same direction. Repeat this step to make a total of 4 sections. Press the seams open.

3. Sew together 2 Flying Geese sections so that the geese point toward each other. Repeat this step to make a second Flying Geese border strip. Both borders should measure 6" × 33½" unfinished. *Figure D*

Figure D: Make 2 Flying Geese borders.

Half-Square Triangle Chevron Borders

1. Pair the following squares right sides together: 4 yellow/green, 4 green/orange, 4 green/pink, 4 green/white.

2. Refer to Making Half-Square Triangles (page 123) to make 48 half-square triangle (HST) units.

3. If necessary, trim each HST unit to 3¼″ × 3¼″.

4. Arrange 24 HST units in 2 rows of 12, forming a chevron design as shown. Sew together to make a border strip. Press the seams open. Repeat this step to make a second border. Each should measure 6″ × 33½″ unfinished. *Figure E*

Figure E: Make 2 HST chevron borders.

Orange Peel Blocks

1. Refer to Piecing Curves (page 117) to sew a background D piece to a side of a C piece. Press the seams open. Sew a second piece D to the opposite side. Press the seams open.

2. Repeat Step 1 to make a total of 16 Orange Peel units.

3. Sew 4 Orange Peel units of the same color together as shown to make an Orange Peel block. Press the seams open. Repeat this step to make a total of 4 Orange Peel blocks that each measure 6″ × 6″ unfinished. *Figure F*

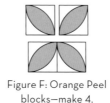

Figure F: Orange Peel blocks—make 4.

TIP: Alternatively, you could appliqué the Orange Peel blocks. Simply appliqué 4 C pieces onto a 6″ × 6″ square using the appliqué method described in Border 3, Flower Blocks (page 71).

4. Sew an Orange Peel block to each end of the 2 HST chevron borders. Press the seams open.

Border 2

FABRIC

Pink, green, yellow, and orange prints: a variety to total ½ yard

White: 1 yard

CUT

Pink, green, yellow, and orange prints

- Cut 3 strips 2½" × 16" from each color for a total of 12 strips.

White

- Cut 12 strips 2½" × width of fabric; then cut 2 strips 2½" × 16" from each for a total of 24 strips.

- Cut 4 squares 3¼" × 3¼".

SEW

Squares-on-Point Blocks

1. Sew together the 2½" × 16" strips into sets of 3—white, print, white. Press the seams toward the white fabric. Make a total of 12 strip sets.

2. From the strip sets, cut 68 rectangles 2½" × 6½".

3. Sew together 17 rectangles, staggering them as shown, to set the colored squares on point. Press the seams to the side. Repeat this step to make a total of 4 border strips. *Figure G*

Figure G

> **TIP:** For perfect colored triangles at the end of each border strip, sew the rectangles together with a *generous* ¼" seam allowance. Then press seams to the sides.

4. Square up each border strip to 3¼" × 44½", making sure to allow for a ¼" seam allowance at the point of each print square. *Figure H*

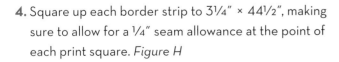

Figure H: Make 4.

5. Sew a 3¼" × 3¼" white square to each end of 2 border strips.

Border 3

FABRIC

Pink, green, yellow, and orange prints: a variety to total 3 yards, including at least ¼ yard each orange and pink and ⅛ yard green for flower blocks.

White: 3 yards

Lightweight fusible interfacing: ⅛ yard

CUT

Flower Blocks

Pink

- Cut 16 strips 2½″ × 5″.

Orange

- Cut 16 strips 2½″ × 5″.

Green

- Cut 4 of Pattern A for flower unit.
- Cut 8 of Pattern F for leaves.
- Cut 4 rectangles 1″ × 5″ for stems.

White

- Cut 4 of Template B.
- Cut 4 squares 12¼″ × 12¼″. Cut 1 of Pattern E from each.
- Cut 4 squares 14″ × 14″; cut in half diagonally once.

Lightweight fusible interfacing

- Cut 8 of Pattern F for leaves.
- Cut 4 rectangles 1″ × 5″ for stems.

Orange Peel Blocks

Pink and orange

- Cut 16 (8 pink and 8 orange) of Pattern C, paying attention to the grainline on the pattern.

White

- Cut 3 strips 3¼″ × width of fabric. From the strips; cut 32 of Pattern D.

Herringbone Border

Pink, orange, yellow, and green

- Cut approximately 32 strips ranging from 1½″ to 3½″ × width of fabric; then cut each in half to make strips approximately 20″ long.

Note: The number of strips needed may vary, depending on how wide you cut the strips. Cut some, sew, and then cut more as needed.

White

- Cut 16 strips 1½″ × width of fabric.

Flower Blocks

1. Repeat Center Medallion, Steps 2 and 3 (page 66) to paper piece 4 Pickle Dish Arcs, using the pink and orange 2½″ × 5″ strips and the A pieces.

2. Repeat Center Medallion, Step 7 (page 66) to sew a white B piece to a Pickle Dish Arc. Then pin and sew an E piece to the opposite side. Press the seams open or toward the white. Repeat this step to make a total of 4 flower blocks.

3. Pin and sew the flower stems and leaves, right sides together, to the corresponding pieces cut from the lightweight fusible interfacing. *Note: If the lightweight fusible interfacing has paper backing, peel it off before pinning.* Cut a slit through only the web and turn each piece right side out, using a turning tool to push out the corners. Finger-press the edges flat.

4. Arrange the flower block as shown and press with a warm iron. Edgestitch around the outer edge of each petal and stem to secure.

5. Square up the blocks as needed to 12″ × 12″ unfinished. *Figure I*

Herringbone Border

1. Sew together enough of the varied-width print strips, staggering the ends in the same direction, to make a 16″-wide strip set. Press the seams open. Repeat to make a total of 8 strip sets, 4 in each direction.

2. From each strip set, cut 4 strips 2¼″ wide at a 45° angle as shown (32 total). *Figure J*

3. Piece together 2 strips cut with the same orientation end to end to make a strip at least 32″ long. Press the seams open. Repeat to make a total of 16 long strips.

4. Sew 2 long strips together lengthwise, making sure the angles point to the center to form a herringbone pattern. Press the seams open. Repeat to make a total of 8 herringbone border strips.

5. Sew a white strip to each long side of the herringbone borders. Press the seams open or to the side. *Figure K*

6. Square up each border strip at the pointed end as shown. *Figure L*

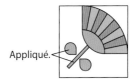

Appliqué.

Figure I: Flower blocks—make 4.

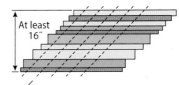

At least 16″

Cut strips at 45° angle.

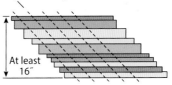

Cut strips at 45° angle.

At least 16″

Figure J: Cut 4 strips 2¼″ wide from each staggered strip set.

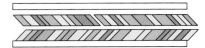

Figure K: Piece strips to make herringbone border.

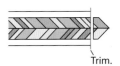

Trim.

Figure L: Trim end with point.

Orange Peel Blocks

Make 4 Orange Peel blocks by repeating Border 1, Orange Peel Blocks, Steps 1–2 (page 68).

Corner Border Assembly

Note: The corner border is oversized and will be trimmed before quilt top assembly.

1. Sew a corner triangle onto a side of the flower block. Press the seam toward the triangle and trim the point of the triangle even with the edge of the block.

2. Sew a second corner triangle to the other side of the flower block. Press the seam toward the triangle.

3. Sew a herringbone border to an Orange Peel block. The herringbone pattern should be pointing toward the block. Press the seam toward the block.

4. Sew a herringbone border to a side of the flower block. The herringbone pattern should be pointed in the direction of the flower stem. Press the seam toward the flower block.

5. Sew the herringbone/Orange Peel unit and the herringbone / flower block units together. Press the seam toward the flower block unit.

6. Repeat Steps 1–5 to make a total of 4 border corners. *Figure M*

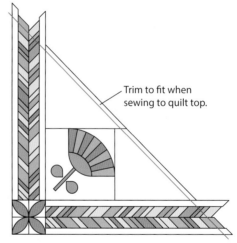

Trim to fit when sewing to quilt top.

Figure M: Make 4 border corners.

QUILT ASSEMBLY

1. Follow the quilt assembly diagram (page 74) to begin assembling the quilt top by sewing the 2 Flying Geese borders to the lower left and upper right sides of the center Pickle Dish medallion. Press.

2. Sew the 2 chevron borders with Orange Peel blocks to the upper left and lower right sides of the Pickle Dish medallion. Press.

3. Repeat Steps 1 and 2 to attach Border 2. Press.

TIP: Match and pin together the centers of the borders and the quilt top. Then match and pin the ends. Pin the rest of the way and sew slowly, being careful not to sew over any points.

4. Measure the quilt top along each side. Trim the long side of the 4 border corners to fit the quilt top. *Figure M*

5. Sew 2 border corners to 2 opposite corners of the quilt top, being careful not to stretch the bias edges. Press. Repeat this step to sew the 2 remaining border corners to the quilt top.

QUILTING AND FINISHING

Layer the backing, batting, and quilt top. Baste.

Quilt and bind using your preferred methods.

Quilt assembly

ABC MEDALLION
WALLHANGING

By Amy Sinibaldi

An alphabet sampler hung on the wall can be both decorative and educational. Use colors pulled from elements in your child's room to make it a truly complementary wallhanging. A smaller-sized project that's perfect for using up those favorite scraps you've been hoarding... this would make a fun, creative escape during naptime.

—Amy

ALL MATERIALS NEEDED FOR QUILT

100% linen evenweave 32: 1 piece at least 12″ × 12″ for center (I used MCG Textiles evenweave in Oyster.)

Gray gingham print: 1/8 yard for borders

Text prints: 1/4 yard total or 1 fat quarter for triangle border and corner squares

Assorted colored scraps: 1/4 yard total for triangle border and appliqués

Cream: 1/4 yard or 1 fat quarter for outer border

Backing: 3/4 yard

Binding: 1/4 yard

Fusible web (17″ wide): 1/2 yard

Batting: 24″ × 24″

Embroidery floss: 12 skeins total

Listed are the colors of Cosmo brand embroidery floss used and their DMC equivalents.

- 533: Pistachio Green (DMC 504)
- 734: Cadet Blue (DMC 930, 311)
- 980: Tiffany Blue (DMC 927)
- 811: Soft Pink (DMC 3689, 818)
- 855: Dark Salmon (DMC 3328)
- 763: Grape Soda (DMC 3041)
- 853: Light Coral (DMC 760)
- 2702: Deep Mustard (DMC 3852, 783)
- 382: Sand (DMC 841, 842)
- 381: Oatmeal (DMC 3864, 842)
- 2111: Cotton Candy Pink (DMC 151)
- 2118: Grass Green (DMC 3347)

FABRIC, CUTTING, AND CONSTRUCTION (BY BORDER)

Note: All seam allowances are 1/4″.

Copy the Triangle and Triangle Ender patterns (pullout page P1), trace them onto template plastic, and cut them out to create the templates.

Center Medallion

FABRIC

Linen evenweave 32: 1 piece at least 12″ × 12″

Embroidery floss

SEW

1. Cross-stitch the design (below) centered on the linen. Refer to the photo (above) for color placement or make it your own. Use 3 strands of floss and "stitch over 3" for all cross-stitching. Use 2 strands of floss to embroider the leaves, using split stitch and lazy daisies.

2. Using a quilter's square ruler, center the completed cross-stitch design and trim to 9¼″ × 9¼″.

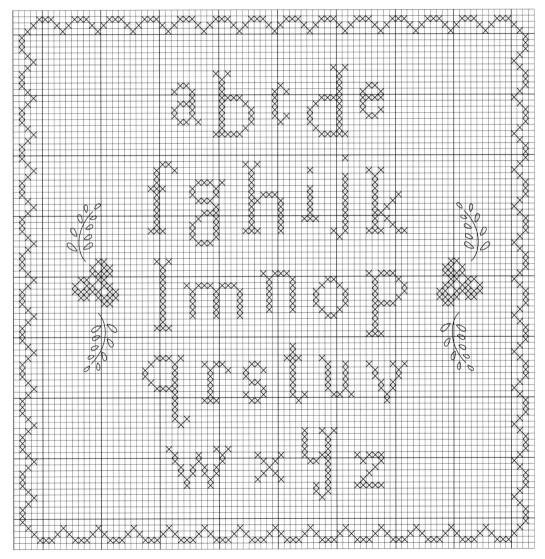

Medallion design

Border 1

FABRIC

Gray gingham print: 1″ × width of fabric strip

CUT

Gray gingham print: Cut 4 strips 1″ × 10¼″ for inner border.

SEW

1. Sew a gray 1″ × 10¼″ strip to each side of the center medallion. Trim the strips even with the top and bottom of the center medallion.

2. Sew a gray 1″ × 10¼″ strip to the top and bottom of the center medallion.

Border 2

FABRIC

Text and colored fabrics:
28 assorted scraps each about 3″ × 3″

CUT

Text

- Cut 20 triangles using the Triangle template.

- Cut 8 triangle enders using the Triangle Ender template.

Assorted colored scraps

- Cut 24 triangles using the Triangle template.

SEW

1. Arrange and sew a border strip of triangles as follows: ender, 5 colored triangles alternating with 4 text triangles, ender. Repeat to make a second border strip. *Figure A*

2. Arrange and sew a border strip of triangles as follows: ender, 7 colored triangles alternating with 6 text triangles, ender. Repeat to make a second border strip.

3. Sew the shorter border strips to the sides of the quilt top. Trim the strips even with the top and bottom. *Figure B*

4. Sew the longer border strips to the top and bottom of the quilt top.

5. Trim to 14½″ × 14½″.

Figure A

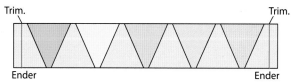

Figure B: Triangle border

Border 3

FABRIC

Gray gingham print: 1 strip about 2½″ × width of fabric

CUT

Gray gingham print: Cut 4 strips 1″ × 15½″.

SEW

1. Sew a gray 1″ × 15½″ strip to each side of the quilt top. Trim the strips even with the top and bottom.

2. Sew a gray 1″ × 15½″ strip to the top and bottom.

Border 4

FABRIC

Cream: 1 fat quarter

Text: 4 scraps, each at least 3½″ × 3½″

Assorted colored scraps: each at least 2″ × 3″

Fusible web: ½ yard

CUT

Cream

- Cut 4 strips 3″ × 15½″ for outer border.

Text

- Cut 4 squares 3″ × 3″ for corner blocks.

Assorted colored scraps

Note: First follow the manufacturer's instructions to apply fusible web to the wrong side of all scraps to be used for appliqué.

- Using the Leaf pattern (pullout page P1), cut 16 leaves and 16 reversed leaves from scraps backed with fusible web for appliqué.

- Using the Circle pattern (pullout page P1), cut 4 circles from scraps backed with fusible web for appliqué on the corner blocks.

> **TIP:** Try cutting the leaves from already-pieced scraps or sew 2 scraps together.

SEW

*Do **not** appliqué the motifs onto the strips yet.*

1. Sew a 3″ × 15½″ strip of cream fabric to each side of the quilt top.

2. Sew a 3″ × 3″ square of text fabric to each end of a 3″ × 15½″ cream strip. Repeat this step to make a second border strip.

3. Sew the longer border strips to the top and bottom of the quilt.

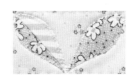

QUILTING AND FINISHING

1. Layer the backing, batting, and quilt top. Baste.

2. Quilt as desired, leaving the areas where appliqués will be placed unquilted.

3. Follow the quilt assembly diagram (below) to center a circle on each corner block. Evenly space 4 pairs of leaves within each outer border.

4. Following the manufacturer's instructions, fuse the appliqués in place.

5. Stitch around the appliqués through all layers to secure. This will also quilt these areas.

6. Bind using your preferred methods.

Quilt assembly

GRAPHICAL MODERN
MEDALLION

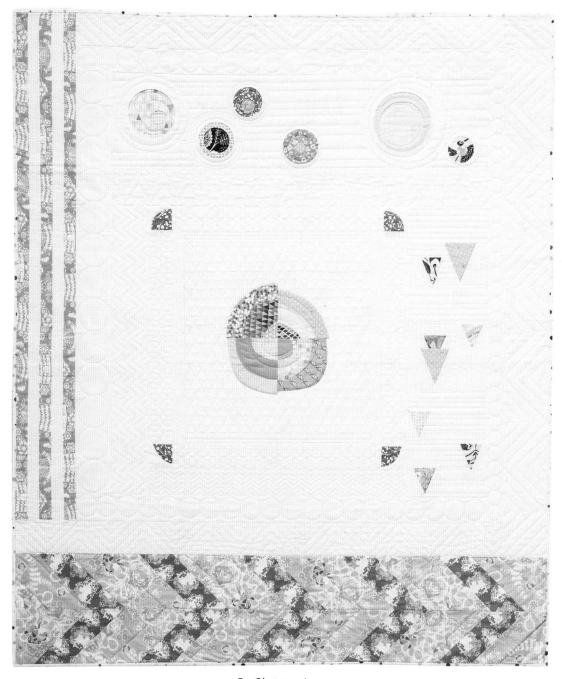

By Christina Lane

For me, nothing feels more modern than simple geometric shapes surrounded by lots of white space. Graphical Modern Medallion allows you to have fun with precious fabrics and gives you lots of room for creative quilting.

—Christina

ALL MATERIALS NEEDED FOR QUILT

Note: This quilt was constructed with asymmetrical borders and partial seam piecing so that the longer borders can be cut from width-of-fabric strips. As long as you have at least 42½" usable width of fabric, the borders will not have to be pieced or cut on the lengthwise grain.

Background: 3 yards*

Assorted prints: ¼ yard for striped side border* and ½ yard each of 2 contrasting prints for chevron border

Fat eighths: 12 different prints or solids for use in center medallion, quarter-circle border, triangle border, and faced-circles border (This is a great quilt to use larger scraps.)

Batting: 56" × 62"

Backing: 3¼ yards

Binding: ½ yard

Foundation paper, such as Carol Doak's Foundation Paper or Simple Foundations Translucent Vellum Paper

* Requires 42½" usable width of fabric or additional yardage to piece to needed length.

FABRIC, CUTTING, AND CONSTRUCTION (BY BORDER)

All seam allowances are ¼" unless otherwise noted. Press the seam allowances to the side as desired, unless otherwise noted. For this quilt top, you will first cut and assemble all the borders and then sew all the borders to the top.

Copy the patterns (pullout page P2) and cut them out to create paper foundations for Blocks 1, 2, 3A, 3B, and 3C and the circle patterns. You will need 1 paper copy of each foundation pattern and 1 template for each circle.

TIP: If you will be using just one fabric for the background, cut all of the strips first, label them, and then cut the smaller pieces from the remaining fabric. This ensures the best use of the background fabric yardage. The prints require much smaller pieces, so the print yardages listed will not be completely used up in each section.

Center Medallion

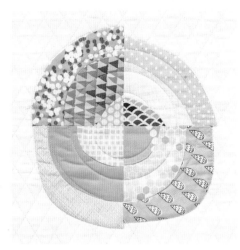

FABRIC

Background: ³/₈ yard

Prints*/solid colors: 3–12 fat eighths or large scraps

* These prints come from the 12 fat eighths listed in All Materials Needed for Quilt.

CUT

Background

- Cut 1 strip 9½″ × width of fabric; then cut 4 squares 9½″ × 9½″.

Prints/solid colors

- Cut 4 squares 6″ × 6″ for outer quarter-circles.

- Cut 4 squares 5″ × 5″ for middle quarter-circles.

- Cut 4 squares 4″ × 4″ for inner quarter-circles.

> **NOTE:** Use 3–12 different fabrics for your desired look.

SEW

The center medallion is composed of 4 quarter-circle blocks that are pieced improvisationally.

1. For the first block, select a 6″ × 6″ outer, 5″ × 5″ middle, and 4″ × 4″ inner square.

2. Place the middle square right side up on a cutting mat. Place the inner square right side up on top of it with the left and bottom edges extending out ¼″ beyond the sides of the middle square. With a rotary cutter, cut a curve through both pieces of fabric as shown, making a rough quarter-circle shape. *Figure A*

Figure A

> **TIP:** The gentler the curve, the easier to sew, but the less dramatic it will be in the finished block. Offsetting the square ¼″ on 2 sides adds a seam allowance, which will make sewing the pieces together a little easier. So cut the curve as desired. Don't be too worried about the ends not meeting completely or the block looking a little wonky— extra fabric is allowed for squaring up later.

3. Discard the concave (curved-in) piece from the inner square and the convex (curved-out) piece from the middle square. *Figure B*

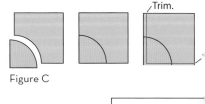

Figure B

4. Refer to Piecing Curves (page 117) to sew the convex and concave pieces right sides together. With a hot iron, press the seam allowance toward the convex piece. *Note: It is okay if the quarter-circle unit is not quite square, but squaring up the 2 pieced edges of the unit now may make the following steps easier. Figure C*

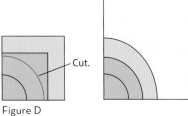

Figure C

5. Repeat Steps 2–4, layering the previously pieced unit onto the 6″ × 6″ outer square and then onto the 9½″ × 9½″ background square. *Figure D*

6. Repeat Steps 2–5 with the remaining pieces to make a total of 4 quarter-circle blocks.

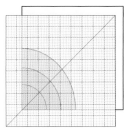

Figure D

7. Square all the blocks to 8½″ × 8½″, removing just enough fabric to square up first from the 2 pieced edges and removing the bulk of the fabric from the background fabric edges. *Figure E*

8. Sew together in 2 rows of 2 quarter-circle blocks to form a circle. Pin to match the center seam. Press all seam allowances open. *Figure F*

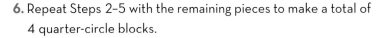

Figure E

Border 1

FABRIC

Background: ⅛ yard

CUT

Background: Cut 2 strips 1½″ × width of fabric; then cut into 2 strips 1½″ × 16½″ and 2 strips 1½″ × 18½″.

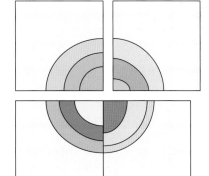

Figure F : Center medallion

Border 2: Quarter-Circle Border

FABRIC

Background: ¼ yard

Print: 1 fat eighth or large scrap

CUT

Background

- Cut 2 strips 2½" × width of fabric; then cut into 4 strips 2½" × 18½".

- Cut 4 squares 3½" × 3½".

Print

- Cut 4 squares 3" × 3".

SEW

1. Repeat Center Medallion, Steps 2–4 (pages 83 and 84) to create 4 quarter-circle blocks using the 4 background squares and 4 print squares.

2. Square up each block to 2½" × 2½".

3. Sew a quarter-circle block as a cornerstone to each end of a 2½" × 18½" background strip as shown. Repeat this step to make a total of 2. *Figure G*

Figure G: Make 2.

Border 3: Triangle Border

FABRIC

Background: ¾ yard

Prints: 5–8 fat eighths
or 8 scraps 3" × 3" to 4" × 5"

CUT

Background

- Cut 1 strip 2¾" × width of fabric; then cut 1 strip 2¾" × 22½" for bottom border.

- Cut 1 strip 3½" × width of fabric; then cut 1 strip 3½" × 24¾" for left border.

- Cut 1 strip 3½" × width of fabric; then cut 1 strip 3½" × 32½" for top border.

- Cut 1 strip 7½" × width of fabric; then cut 2 strips 7½" × 3½" and 1 strip 7½" × 2¼".

Use the remaining fabric to paper piece the triangle blocks.

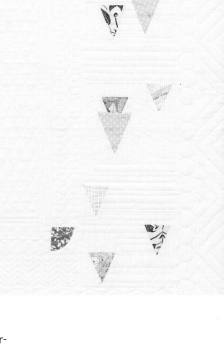

SEW

Refer to Foundation Paper Piecing (page 124) as needed.

1. Paper piece Blocks 1, 2, 3A, 3B, and 3C using the print scraps for the triangles. *Figure H*

2. Trim the paper-pieced blocks to a ¼″ seam allowance and remove the foundation paper.

3. Assemble Block 3 by sewing Block 3A to Block 3B and then sewing Block 3A/B to 3C as shown in the border assembly diagram. *Figure I*

4. Sew a 7½″ × 3½″ strip to Block 1 and the other 7½″ × 3½″ strip to Block 2 as shown. Sew the 7½″ × 2¼″ strip to Block 3 as shown. *Figure I*

5. Sew Blocks 1, 2, and 3 together as shown to form the triangle border strip. *Figure I*

Block 3A   Block 3B   Block 3C

Figure H

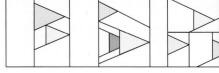

Figure I: Triangle border assembly

Border 4: Faced Circles

The top border strip has cut-out circles that are faced, or lined, so that the print fabrics underneath show through.

FABRIC

Background: ⅞ yard

Print: 5–12 fat eighths or large scraps

CUT

Background

- Cut 1 strip 2″ × width of fabric; then cut 1 strip 2″ × 37¾″ for right border.

- Cut 1 strip 2½″ × width of fabric; then cut 1 strip 2½″ × 35½″ for bottom border.

- Cut 1 strip 3½″ × width of fabric; then cut 1 strip 3½″ × 35¾″ for left border.

Outer circle print

Inner circle print

Block background

Cut the remaining background and print fabrics according to the chart:

BLOCK #		BACKGROUND FABRIC			PRINT FABRIC		COMPLETED BLOCK SIZE (including seam allowance)
		Block background cut size	FACING CUT SIZE		For outer print circle:	For inner print circle:	
			For background circle:	For outer print circle:			
1		7½" × 9½"	6" × 6"	3½" × 3½"	5" × 5"	2½" × 2½"	6½" × 8½"
2	A	9½" × 9½"	4½" × 4½"	3¼" × 3¼"	3½" × 3½"	2¼" × 2¼"	8½" × 8½"
	B		5" × 5"	4" × 4"	4" × 4"	3" × 3"	
3		7½" × 9½"	5" × 5"	3" × 3"	4" × 4"	2" × 2"	6½" × 8½"
4		9½" × 9½"	7" × 7"	6" × 6"	6" × 6"	5" × 5"	8½" × 8½"
5		5½" × 9½"	4¼" × 4¼"	3" × 3"	3¼" × 3¼"	2" × 2"	4½" × 8½"

SEW

Sew Blocks 1–5 a block at a time using the following method. Use the cutting chart (above) and the circle chart below to organize the pieces for each block. There are no exact placement directions; simply eyeball where to place the circles within the blocks, remembering to leave enough room for a seam allowance at the edges.

BLOCK #	CIRCLE SIZES TO DRAW	
	For background circle:	For outer print circle:
1	4"	1½"
2A	2½"	1¼"
2B	3"	2"
3	3"	1"
4	5"	4"
5	2¼"	1"

TIP: Place the fabrics over the circle patterns on a light table or taped to a window during daylight hours. Alternatively, make templates for each circle size and trace around them.

1. Place a background circle facing on top of the corresponding block background, right sides together, where you would like the larger print circle to be. Pin together and then trace the corresponding-sized background circle in the center of the facing square.

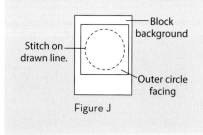

Stitch on drawn line.

Block background

Outer circle facing

Figure J

2. Stitch on the drawn line through both layers of fabric. Backstitch at the end to secure the stitches. *Figure J*

3. Make a cut in the center of the sewn circle through both layers. Cut away all around the inside of the circle, leaving a ¼" seam allowance. Clip into the seam allowance at ¼" (or less) intervals, just to the stitching but not through it. *Figure K*

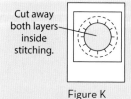

Cut away both layers inside stitching.

Figure K

4. Push the facing through the clipped circle so both layers are wrong sides together. Finger-press the finished edge; then press with a hot iron. *Figure L*

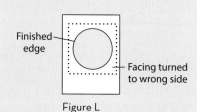

Finished edge

Facing turned to wrong side

Figure L

5. Repeat Steps 1–3 with the outer print facing (cut from background fabric) and the outer print circle square to make a finished-edge circle opening in the outer print fabric square. *Figure M*

TIPS: For smaller circles, try shortening the stitch length on your sewing machine. If the fabric shifts behind a finished circle, use a fabric glue stick to hold it in place.

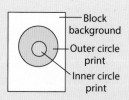

Cut away both layers inside stitching.

Figure M

6. Place the finished outer print circle on top of the corresponding inner print square, both right sides up. Stitch around the circle, ⅛" from the edge, through all 3 layers, securing the inner print square as the bottom layer.

7. Do not backstitch—instead, leave the long tail of threads. Pull both threads to the wrong side, double knot, and cut off the excess thread. Trim away the facing and inner print to a ¼" seam allowance of the circle, if desired.

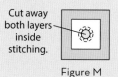

Block background

Outer circle print

Inner circle print

Figure N: Faced circle block

8. Repeat Steps 6 and 7 to sew the faced print circle to the background faced circle from Step 4. *Figure N*

9. Square up the block according to the size on the cutting chart (page 87).

10. Repeat Steps 1–9 to make a total of 5 faced circle blocks according to the sizes on the charts.

11. Sew the blocks together as shown to make the top border strip. *Figure O*

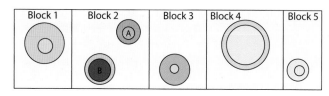

Figure O: Faced circle border assembly

Border 5: Striped Border

FABRIC

Background: ½ yard*

Print: ¼ yard*

Both fabrics require at least a 42½" usable width of fabric; otherwise you will need more to piece at least this length.

CUT

Background

- Cut 2 strips 1½" × width of fabric for left striped border (5C).

- Cut 1 strip 2½" × width of fabric; then cut 1 strip 2½" × 37" for top border (5A).

- Cut 2 strips 3¼" × width of fabric for the top border (5B) and the bottom border (5D).

- Cut 1 strip 4½" × width of fabric for the right border (5E).

Print

- Cut 3 strips 1½" × width of fabric for left striped border (5C).

SEW

1. Sew together the 1½" × width of fabric print and background strips lengthwise, alternating print, background, print, background, print.

2. Square up the ends, trimming off any longer ends. Any remaining excess length will be trimmed when attaching the borders.

Border 6: Chevron Border

FABRIC

Print A: ⅓ yard

Print B: ¼ yard

CUT

Print A: Cut 2 strips 5" × width of fabric.

Print B: Cut 2 strips 2½" × width of fabric.

SEW

1. Place the 2 A strips wrong sides together, matching the ends and sides. Pin in the middle of the strip along the length to hold them in place. Cut off the selvages from both ends if you haven't already done so.

2. Mark 10½" in from an end of the strip. Using a ruler with a 45° line, line up the 45° line on the ruler with a long side of the strips and the 10½" mark. Make a 45° angled cut in the fabric strip.

3. Set aside the 2 angled 10½" pieces for the ends of the border.

4. Keeping the ruler at a 45° angle, move it over 4½" as shown and cut. Repeat to cut a total of 8 pieces 4½" wide and 4 end pieces. *Figure P*

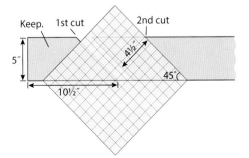

Figure P: Cutting wide pieces

5. Separate the cut pieces into the group that was cut right side up and the group that was cut right side down.

6. Repeat Step 1 with the 2 B strips.

7. Line up the 45° angle on the ruler with the long edge of the strips and cut the end of the fabric at a 45° angle. Discard these 2 pieces.

8. Repeat Step 4, but this time cut a total of 10 pieces 5″ wide. Separate the pieces as in Step 5. *Figure Q*

9. Arrange the A and B pieces from each pile into the upper and lower halves of the chevron border as shown. The B pieces will be rotated so that the 45° cuts are at the top and bottom edges of the strips. When handling the pieces, be careful not to distort the bias edges. *Figure R*

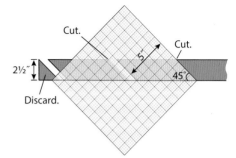

Figure Q: Cutting narrow pieces

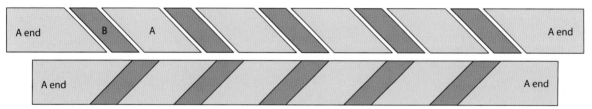

Figure R

10. Sew the A and B pieces together in 2 rows, offsetting the pieces ¼″ so they align when sewn. Press the seam allowances in opposite directions in each row.

11. Sew the 2 rows together, matching seams at the center, to complete the border strip. Press the seam allowance open. *Figure S*

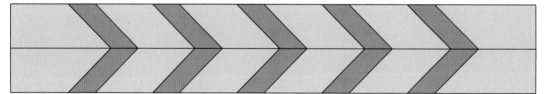

Figure S: Chevron border

TIP: Pin through the seam allowance on each side of the angled seams to prevent shifting when sewing.

QUILT ASSEMBLY

LAST BORDER SEWN TO TOP	YOUR QUILT SHOULD MEASURE (including seam allowance)
Center medallion	16½″ × 16½″
Border 1	18½″ × 18½″
Border 2	22½″ × 22½″
Border 3	32½″ × 27¾″
Border 4	37″ × 37¾″
Border 5	46″ × 54¼″

Refer to the quilt assembly diagram (page 92) as needed.

Border 1

1. Sew a 1½″ × 16½″ background strip to the top and bottom of the center medallion.

2. Sew a 1½″ × 18½″ strip to each side of the center medallion.

Border 2

1. Sew a 2½″ × 18½″ background strip to the top and bottom of the main piece.

2. Sew the borders with cornerstones to each side of the main piece, being sure to pin the seam allowances at the cornerstones before sewing.

Border 3

1. Sew the 2¾″ × 22½″ background strip to the bottom of the main piece.

2. Sew the 3½″ × 24¾″ background strip to the left side of the main piece.

3. Sew the triangle border to the right side of the main piece. Press the seam allowance toward the main piece to reduce bulk.

4. Sew a 3½″ × 32½″ background strip to the top of the main piece.

Border 4

1. Sew the circle border to the top of the main piece. Press the seam allowance toward the main piece to reduce bulk.

2. Sew the 3½″ × 35¾″ background strip to the left side of the main piece.

3. Sew the 2½″ × 35½″ background strip to the bottom of the main piece.

4. Sew the 2″ × 37¾″ background strip to the right side of the main piece.

Border 5

> **NOTE:** Pay attention to the partial-seam piecing used when attaching these borders.

1. Sew the 2½″ × 37″ background strip (5A) to the top of the main piece. Press the seam allowance toward the strip to reduce bulk.

2. Starting on the left side of the quilt top, sew the 3¼″ × width of fabric background strip (5B) to the top of the strip sewn in Step 1, stopping a few inches from the end.

3. Sew the striped border (5C) to the left side of the piece. Trim the top and bottom of the border even with the main piece.

4. Sew the 3¼″ × width of fabric background strip (5D) to the bottom of the main piece. Trim the border even with the sides of the main piece.

5. Pin the loose end of Border 5B back on itself so it is out of the way. Sew the 4½″ × width of fabric strip (5E) to the right side of the piece. Press. Unpin the end of Border 5B and continue stitching it across the top of the quilt. Trim it even with the right side of the main piece.

Border 6

1. Fold the chevron border in half lengthwise to find its center. Mark with a pin.

2. Repeat Step 1 with the main piece.

3. Matching the centers, pin along the length of the chevron border andthe main piece, and then sew together.

4. Trim the excess chevron border from each side, squaring up to the sides of the quilt top.

QUILTING AND FINISHING

Layer the backing, batting, and quilt top. Baste.

Quilt and bind using your preferred methods.

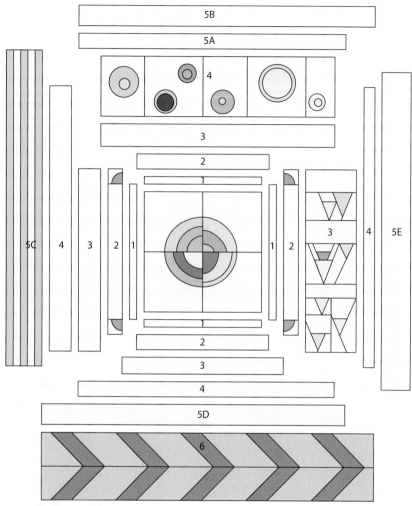

Quilt assembly

Christina's Medallion Tip

If you have pieced borders, piece all of those first before assembling the quilt; doing so will save you from making mistakes. Focusing on too many tasks at once can lead to headaches in the long run. Take your time, check the seam allowance, and square the blocks where needed so that the borders are always just the right size when sewing them around the medallion.

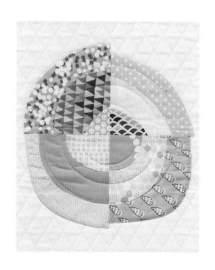

ONE STEP
AT A TIME

By Melissa Richie

The majority of the fabrics used in this quilt are from Michael Miller and Robert Kaufman.

In life, we often face difficult situations. How do we get through them? By taking one step at a time. Just like this quilt, a sampling of different chevron designs, you can make it if you just take it one step at a time.

—Melissa

ALL MATERIALS NEEDED FOR QUILT

White solid: 2 yards

Aqua solid: 1⅛ yards

Ice blue print: ⅓ yard

Navy blue prints: a variety totaling at least 2 yards

Green prints: a variety totaling at least 1 yard, including ⅓ yard of 1 print for the quarter-circle blocks

Binding: ½ yard

Backing: 1⅞ yards 108"-wide fabric, or 3⅝ yards standard quilting-width fabric

Batting: 62" × 62"

Card stock or Templar (heat-resistant plastic for hexagon template)

FABRIC, CUTTING, AND CONSTRUCTION (BY BORDER)

Note: All seam allowances are ¼". Press seam allowances to the darker fabric unless stated otherwise.

Copy the patterns (pullout page P2) and cut each from card stock or Templar to create Templates A, B, C, and D. You will need 1 copy of each.

Center Medallion

FABRIC

White: 1 square at least 12½" × 12½"

Navy blue, green, and ice blue prints: scraps at least 3" × 3"

CUT

White: Cut 1 square 12½" × 12½".

Navy blue, green, and ice blue prints: Using Template A, cut hexagons from every colored print you will use. Make as many or as few as you like. *(Note: I used 14 prints.)*

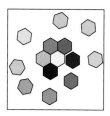

Figure A

SEW

1. Starch each hexagon. Wrap a hexagon, right side out, around the Template B made from card stock or Templar to create a ¼" turned edge. Press a crease along each edge with a hot iron and remove the template. Repeat for all the hexagons.

2. Arrange the hexagons on the 12½" square, spiraling out from the center. Leave a ¼" seam allowance around the edges.

3. Pin or glue baste each hexagon in place. Then appliqué using your favorite method. *Figure A*

TIP: I used an invisible thread and the blind hem stitch on my machine. You could also topstitch around each hexagon or hand stitch in place.

Border 1

FABRIC

Aqua: ⅛ yard

CUT

Aqua: Cut 2 strips 1½" × width of fabric; then cut into 2 strips 1½" × 12½" and 2 strips 1½" × 14½".

Border 2

FABRIC

White: ⅜ yard

Navy blue: ¼ yard

Ice blue: ⅓ yard

CUT

White and ice blue

From each fabric:

- Cut 1 strip 6″ × width of fabric; then cut 8 rectangles 4½″ × 6″. Cut 4 of the rectangles from 1½″ down the left side diagonally to 4½″ down on the right side to yield 8 A pieces (white) and 8 C pieces (ice blue) as shown. *Figure B*

- Cut the remaining 4 rectangles from 1½″ down the *right* side diagonally to 4½″ down on the left side to yield 8 D pieces (white) and 8 F pieces (ice blue) as shown. *Figure C*

From white only:

- Cut 1 strip 6½″ × 26; then cut into 4 squares 6½″ × 6½″. Cut the squares from 1½″ down on the right side diagonally to 1½″ from the bottom left to yield 4 G triangles as shown. Discard the smaller triangles. *Figure D*

From ice blue only:

- Cut 2 squares 5″ × 5″; then cut those in half diagonally once to yield 4 half-square triangles I. *Figure E*

Navy blue

- Cut 4 strips 1½″ × width of fabric; then cut into 16 B strips 1½″ × 6½″ and 4 E strips 1½″ × 8½″.

SEW

1. Sew A to B and trim the sides even. Sew B to C, offsetting the pieces so they will align. Trim ¼″ off each side to make the block 4″ × 6½″. Make 8. *Figure F*

> **TIP:** Make a trimming template with the position of the B strip marked so you can trim each block exactly the same and match the points easily later.

2. Sew D to B; then sew B to F as in Step 1. Trim ¼″ off each side to make the block 4″ × 6½″. Make 8. *Figure F*

Figure B: Cut 4 sets.

Figure C: Cut 4 sets.

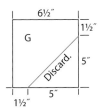

Figure D: Cut 4.

Figure E: Cut 2.

3. Sew G to E and E to I. Trim to 6½″ × 6½″ square. Make 4. *Figure F*

4. Sew together 4 blocks as shown, making a zigzag design. Repeat to make a total of 4 border strips. *Figure G*

5. Sew a 6½″ × 6½″ corner block to each end of 2 border strips. *Figure H*

Figure F: Block assembly

Figure G: Border 2 top and bottom

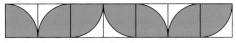

Figure H: Border 2 sides

Border 3

FABRIC

Navy blue: ¼ yard

CUT

Navy blue: Cut 4 strips 1½″ × width of fabric; then cut into 2 strips 1½″ × 26½″ and 2 strips 1½″ × 28½″.

Border 4

FABRIC

White: ⅓ yard

Green: ⅓ yard

CUT

White: Cut 2 strips 4½″ × width of fabric; then cut into 15 squares 4½″ × 4½″. Using Template C, cut 15 concave (curved-in) pieces.

Green: Cut 2 strips 4½″ × width of fabric; then cut into 15 squares 4½″ × 4½″. Using Template D, cut 15 convex (curved-out) pieces.

SEW

1. Sew pieces C to pieces D (refer to Piecing Curves, page 117). Press the seams toward the green. Trim to 4½″ × 4½″ square if needed.

Quarter-circle block

2. Sew together 7 quarter-circle blocks as shown, alternating the direction of the blocks for the left side border. Then sew together 8 quarter-circle blocks as shown for the top border.

Border 4 assembly—left side

Border 4 assembly—top

Border 5

Navy blue: ¼ yard

Navy blue: Cut 4 strips 1½″ × width of fabric; then cut into 2 strips 1½″ × 32½″ and 2 strips 1½″ × 34½″.

Border 6

White: 1 fat eighth

Aqua: ⅓ yard

Green: a variety of 1½″–2″ × width of fabric strips to total 1 yard

White: Cut into 2 squares 9″ × 9″; then cut each in half diagonally to yield 4 border corner triangles.

Aqua: Cut 7 strips 1½″ × width of fabric. Further cut 1 strip into 4 strips 1½″ × 6½″.

Green: Cut at least 15 strips 1½″–2″ × width of fabric.

1. Choose 4 or 5 green strips of prints that vary in scale. Sew together lengthwise to make a long strip set. *Note: You may need to cut and sew more strips if you use more of the narrow strips.* Trim the strip set to 6″ × width of fabric.

2. Sew an aqua 1½″ × width of fabric strip to the top and the bottom of each strip set so it is 8″ × width of fabric.

3. Repeat Steps 1 and 2 to make a total of 3 strip sets.

4. Cut a total of 14 strip set segments each 6½″ wide, making sure the cuts are perpendicular to the seams. *Figure I*

TIP: Starching the strip set before you cut will help keep it from warping or stretching.

5. Use the 45° angle line on a ruler to cut 7 segments twice to yield 14 A 6½″ half-square triangles. *Figure J*

6. Use the 45° angle line on a ruler to cut the remaining 7 segments twice in the opposite direction to yield 14 B 6½″ half-square triangles. *Figure K*

7. Arrange 4 A and 3 B triangles, alternating them as shown so the aqua borders create a zigzag pattern. *Figure L*

8. Sew the triangles together to make a border strip, being careful to offset the corners ¼″ to account for the seam allowance. Sew a short aqua strip to the green side of the A triangle at the end, so

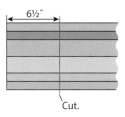

Figure I: Strip set construction

Figure J: Triangle A cutting

Figure K: Triangle B cutting

there is an aqua strip on each end. Trim the row to 4" unfinished, removing the dog-ears. *Figure L*

9. Repeat the previous step with 4 B and 3 A triangles and a short aqua strip to make a border strip. *Figure M*

10. Repeat Steps 7–9 to make another of each type of border strip.

Figure L: Border 6 assembly

Figure M: Border 6 assembly

Border 7

FABRIC

Navy print: ¼ yard

CUT

Navy print: Cut 5 strips 1½" × width of fabric; then sew end to end to make a long strip. Then cut into 2 strips 1½" × 41½" and 2 strips 1½" × 43½".

Border 8

FABRIC

Aqua: ¼ yard

CUT

Aqua: Cut 3 strips 1½" × width of fabric (or piece together leftover strip scraps). Sew end to end to make a long strip. Then cut into 1 strip 1½" × 43½" and 1 strip 1½" × 44½".

Border 9: Palace Steps

FABRIC

White: ½ yard

Navy blue prints (4 different values—light, medium light, medium dark, dark): ¼ yard each

Aqua: 1 strip 1½" × 12½" for corner block

CUT

White

- Cut 1 half-square triangle 8½" for the corner block.

- Cut 2 strips 3½" × 30".

- Cut 2 strips 1½" × 37".

- Cut 2 strips 2½" × 37".

Note: Cut the triangle first from yardage, and then cut strips from remaining yardage to use fabric more efficiently.

Navy blue prints

- Cut 1 strip 5½" × 30" for Palace Steps borders and 1 piece 3½" × 5" for corner block from light fabric (A).

- Cut 1 strip 5½" × 37" for Palace Steps borders and 1 piece 2¼" × 8" for corner block from medium-light fabric (B).

- Cut 1 strip 5½" × 37" for Palace Steps borders and 1 piece 2" × 11" for corner block from medium-dark fabric (C).

- Cut 1 strip 5½" × 30" and 1 strip 1½" × 12½" for corner block from dark fabric (D).

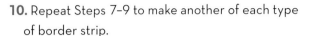

SEW

1. Sew the long A navy strip to a corresponding-length white strip lengthwise to make strip set A. Repeat this step with the long D navy strip to make strip set D. *Figure N*

2. Sew a corresponding-length white strip to each side of the long B and C navy strips as shown to make strip sets B and C.

3. Cut strip sets A and D each into 10 strips 2½" × 8½" and 2 strips 1½" × 8½".

4. Cut strip sets B and C into 22 strips 1½" × 8½".

5. For the left border, start with a 1½"-wide A strip and add the following strips in order: B/C/D/C/B/A, ending with a 2½"-wide A strip and making sure to orient the strips as shown. *Figure P*

6. Continue sewing strips in the same order until you have used 5 of the 2½"-wide A strips and 5 D strips. Then sew a B strip, a C strip, and a D strip 1½" wide as shown to complete the border. *Figures P & Q*

7. For the top border, start with a 1½"-wide D strip and add the following strips in order: C/B/A/B/C/D, ending with a 2½"-wide D strip and making sure to orient the strips as shown. Repeat until you have used 5 of the 2½"-wide D strips. Then sew a C strip, a B strip, and an A strip 1½" wide as shown to complete the border. *Figures R & S*

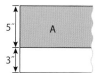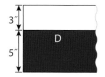

Figure N: Strip sets A and D. *Note: Finished measurements shown.*

Figure O: Strip sets B and C. *Note: Finished measurements shown.*

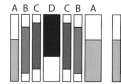

Figure P: Palace Steps assembly

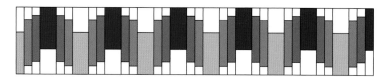

Figure Q: Completed Palace Steps left border

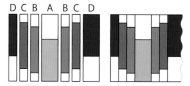

Figure R: Palace Steps assembly

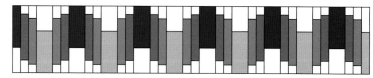

Figure S: Completed Palace Steps top border

Palace Steps Corner Block Construction

1. Cut an 8½" × 8½" square of paper and draw a diagonal centerline.

2. Sew the aqua strip to the navy D strip. Press the seam open.

3. Glue the sewn strips right side up onto the paper, with the seamline directly on top of the drawn line and oriented as shown.

TIP: There are a number of ways to create the corner, but I found foundation paper piecing (page 124) to be the easiest.

4. Sew the navy C strip on top of the D strip, right sides together. Press.

5. Repeat Step 4 to sew the navy B and A strips to the foundation paper.

6. Sew the white corner triangle to the other side of the aqua strip. Press.

7. Trim to 8½" × 8½". Remove the paper.

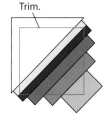

Palace Steps corner block

Border 10

FABRIC

Aqua: ¼ yard

CUT

Aqua

- Cut 6 strips 1⅓" × width of fabric. *Note: You can use aqua scraps from previous borders and only cut 5 strips 1½", making up the rest of the length from scraps.*

- Sew end to end to make a long strip, and then cut 2 strips 1½" × 52½" and 2 strips 1½" × 54½".

QUILT ASSEMBLY

NOTE: As you construct the borders, you may want to assemble the quilt as you go, or you may want to wait until all the borders are complete. I found it easier to attach them as I made them. I starched each border to avoid stretching the fabric. When working with long, skinny borders, place the quilt and the borders flat on a table or the floor to pin or glue baste the fabric together before sewing; this helps avoid warping and misshaping the pieces. It is also helpful to measure the quilt after adding each border to make sure that it is square. If it isn't, you can either take off the border and try again or trim the excess from solid borders.

LAST BORDER SEWN TO TOP	YOUR QUILT SHOULD MEASURE (including seam allowance)
Center medallion	12½" × 12½"
Border 1	14½" × 14½"
Border 2	26½" × 26½"
Border 3	28½" × 28½"
Border 4	32½" × 32½"
Border 5	34½" × 34½"
Border 6	41½" × 41½"
Border 7	43½" × 43½"
Border 8	44½" × 44½"
Border 9	52½" × 52½"
Border 10	54½" × 54½"

1. Sew the shorter Border 1 strips to the top and bottom of the center medallion. Then sew the longer Border 1 strips to the left and right sides.

2. Continue sewing the top and bottom first and then the sides for Borders 2 and 3. Press the seams as you go.

3. For Border 4, sew the shorter strip to the left side of the quilt top and the longer strip to the top of the quilt top.

4. Sew Border 5 using the same method as Border 1 (see Step 1).

5. For Border 6, sew a border strip centered to the left and right sides of the quilt top, referring to the quilt assembly diagram (right) to orient them correctly. Trim the dog-ears even with

   TIP: Measure the quilt top on each side and mark the center; then repeat the process with each Border 6 strip. Match and pin the center of the strip to the center of the quilt top on each side.

the top and bottom of the quilt top, and then add the top and bottom border strips.

6. Sew a white corner setting triangle onto each corner. Press the seams toward the aqua. Square the quilt as needed.

7. Sew Border 7 using the same method as Border 1 (see Step 1).

8. For Border 8, sew the shorter strip to the left side of the quilt top; then sew the longer strip to the top.

9. For Border 9, sew the left border to the left side of the quilt top. Press the seams toward the aqua. Then sew the Palace Steps corner block to the left end of the top border, making sure to orient the corner block correctly. Sew it to the top of the quilt top.

10. Sew Border 10 using the same method as Border 1 (see Step 1).

QUILTING AND FINISHING

Layer the backing, batting, and quilt top. Baste.

Quilt and bind using your preferred methods.

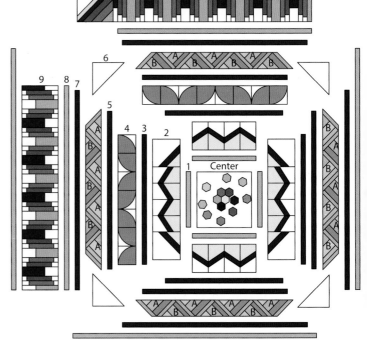

Quilt assembly

ZEN
MEDALLION

By Latifah Saafir

While Zen Medallion has the appearance of a medallion, it is not constructed border by border. Instead, it is sewn in eight wedges that, when put together, form the medallion shape. The medallion uses paper piecing and bias tape appliqué to create a fun, easy-to-sew quilt with big impact.

—Latifah

ALL MATERIALS NEEDED FOR QUILT

Background: 3¼ yards

Navy blue: 16 fat eighths, plus ¼ yard for bias tape appliqué

Peach: 5 fat quarters, or yardage and scraps to total 1¼ yards, plus 2 different ½-yard pieces for bias tape appliqué

Mint: 4 fat eighths and 4 fat quarters, or yardage and scraps to total 1½ yards

Gold: 8 fat eighths, plus ½ yard for bias tape appliqué

Teal: 8 scraps, at least 5″ × 5″, plus ½ yard for bias tape appliqué

Batting: 58″ × 58″

Backing: 3⅛ yards

Binding: 1⅛ yards

1″ (25mm) bias tape maker

Water-soluble fabric marker

Acid-free fabric glue stick

You will need 1 copy each of the Wedge, A/Ar, and B patterns, and 8 copies each of Foundation Patterns 1 and 2. The A/Ar and B patterns do *not* need to have seam allowances added. Copy the patterns (pullout page P1) and cut them out.

CUT

Background

- Use the Wedge pattern to cut 8 wedges from folded fabric, as marked on the pattern.

- Cut 2 squares 16½" × 16½"; then cut in half diagonally once to yield 4 corner setting triangles. (These are cut oversized and will be trimmed later.)

Navy blue

- Cut 8 squares approximately 4" × 4" for Foundation Pattern 1.

- Cut 16 pieces approximately 6" × 7½" for Foundation Pattern 2.

- Cut 8 bias strips 2" wide diagonally across a ¼-yard piece.

Peach

- Cut 8 pieces approximately 4" × 6" for Foundation Pattern 2.

- Cut 8 of Pattern A.

- Cut 4 of Pattern B from folded fabric, as marked on the pattern.

- Cut 8 bias strips 2" wide diagonally across each ½-yard piece (16 total).

Mint

- Cut 16 squares approximately 4" × 4" for Foundation Pattern 1.

- Cut 8 pieces approximately 4" × 6" for Foundation Pattern 2.

- Cut 4 of Pattern B from folded fabric, as marked on the pattern.

Gold

- Cut 8 pieces approximately 4" × 4" and 8 pieces approximately 2½" × 7½" for Foundation Pattern 1.

- Cut 8 squares approximately 6" × 6" for Foundation Pattern 2.

- Cut 8 bias strips 2" wide diagonally across a ½-yard piece.

Teal

- Cut 8 of Pattern A reversed.

- Cut 12 bias strips 2" wide diagonally across a ½-yard piece.

CONSTRUCTION

Refer to Foundation Paper Piecing (page 124) as needed. Seam allowances for paper piecing are ¼″. Bias tape is topstitched as close to the edge as possible. Seam allowances for the final assembly of wedges are ½″.

Making the Bias Tape

Follow the manufacturer's instructions to make each 2″ bias strip into 1″ single-fold bias tape, using a 1″ bias tape maker. Set aside.

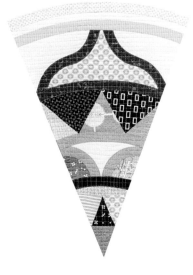

Wedge Assembly

Refer to Latifah's Bias Tape Appliqué (page 109) for how to apply the bias tape.

1. Use a water-soluble fabric marker to transfer all the markings from the Wedge template, including the bias tape marks, to the right side of a background fabric wedge.

2. Paper piece Foundation Patterns 1 and 2 (see Foundation Paper Piecing, page 124) with the navy, gold, and mint pieces. Remove the paper. Set aside. *Figure A*

3. Using a glue stick, lightly glue baste 1 peach A piece and 1 teal A reversed piece in place right side up on the background wedge. *Figure B*

4. See Latifah's Bias Tape Appliqué (page 109) to appliqué a strip of gold bias tape over the curved outer edge of the peach A pieces. Making sure the bias tape covers the edge of the A piece, align the top outside curve with the bias tape mark on the fabric. Stretching the bias tape along the outside curve, topstitch in place, ensuring that the bias tape amply covers the raw edge of the glued piece. Press. Stitch the inside curve of the bias tape. Press. Trim the ends of the bias tape even with the ring line and the sides of the background wedge. *Figure C*

Figure A: Paper piece 8.

Figure B: Glue baste.

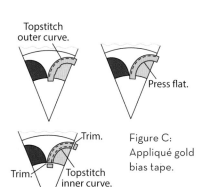

Topstitch outer curve.

Press flat.

Trim.

Trim.

Topstitch inner curve.

Figure C: Appliqué gold bias tape.

5. Repeat Step 4 to appliqué gold bias tape over the curved outer edge of the teal A reversed pieces.

6. Glue baste the B piece in place on the background wedge.

7. Appliqué the teal bias tape to an outer edge of the B piece, starting with the lower curve. This curve changes directions, so while stitching, remember to stretch on the outside curve and relax on the inside curve. Press. Stitch the opposite edge. Press. Trim. Repeat this step to appliqué the opposite side of the B piece. *Figure D*

8. Lightly glue baste Foundation Pattern 1 in place along the placement line on the wedge background. *Figure E*

9. Appliqué the navy blue bias tape over the raw edges of Foundation Pattern 1 and the A/Ar piece. Sew the inside curve first, starting and stopping at the bias tape marks. Press. Sew the outside curve. Press. Trim the ends of the bias tape even with the side of the wedge.

10. Lightly glue baste Foundation Pattern 2 in place along the placement line on the wedge background. *Figure F*

Refer to the quilt assembly diagragm (page 108) or the finished quilt photo for the remaining steps.

11. Appliqué the gold bias tape over the raw edges of Foundation Pattern 2 and the A/Ar piece. Sew the outer curve first, using the triangle points to line up the outer edge of the bias tape. Press. Sew the inside curve. Press. Trim the ends of the bias tape even with the side of the wedge.

12. Appliqué the teal bias tape over the raw edges of Foundation Pattern 2 and the B piece. Sew the inner curve first, using the triangle points to line up the inner edge of the bias tape. Press. Sew the outside curve. Press. Trim the ends of the bias tape even with the side of the wedge.

13. Appliqué the 2 peach bias tapes on rings 4 and 5. Sew the outer curve first. Press. Sew the inner curve. Press. Trim the ends of the bias tape even with the side of the wedge.

14. Cut the background fabric away from behind Foundation Patterns 1 and 2 and the A, Ar, and B pieces, leaving at least a ¼" seam allowance.

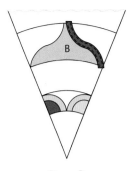

Figure D:
Appliqué teal bias tape.

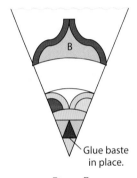

Glue baste
in place.

Figure E

Glue baste
in place.

Figure F

QUILT ASSEMBLY

Seam allowances for the assembly of wedges and corner triangles are ½".

1. Arrange all the wedges and corner triangles on your design wall, following the quilt assembly diagram.

2. Sew the wedges together 2 at a time. Press the seams open.

3. Sew the wedge pairs together to form halves. Press.

4. Sew together 2 halves to make a complete medallion. Press.

5. Sew the corner triangles onto the medallion to make a square. Press the seams open.

6. Square the quilt even with the wedges.

Quilt assembly

QUILTING AND FINISHING

Layer the backing, batting, and quilt top. Baste.

Cut 6 strips 6" × width of fabric from binding fabric for double-fold binding. Sew on with a 1" seam allowance for binding that matches the bias tape appliqué.

Quilt and bind using your preferred methods.

Latifah's Bias Tape Appliqué

Bias tape appliqué takes advantage of the stretch of single-fold bias tape to form curved shapes and bold outlines.

Making single-fold bias tape is easy.

To cut bias strips, simply line up a single layer of fabric with the grid lines on your mat. Using the 45° mark on your ruler, cut a diagonal line across the width of the fabric. Using this line as a guide, move the ruler over and cut the width required for your bias tape appliqué. If you need a longer piece or continuous bias tape, piece the ends by placing the strips right sides together at a 90° angle and sewing across the diagonal. Trim to a ¼" seam allowance.

Press the cut bias strips into single-fold bias tape easily using a bias tape maker. These can be purchased inexpensively and come in ¼", ½", ¾", 1", and 2" sizes. Follow the manufacturer's instructions to see how to feed the fabric through the maker and press the fabric with an iron while pulling the bias tape maker along the length of the bias tape.

The bias tape is topstitched in place along both edges. Place the bias tape with the raw edges facing down (*don't open the folds*). When you begin to stitch down bias tape appliqué on a curve, you can stitch down either the outer or the inner curve first.

If you stitch the outer curve first, stretch the fabric on the outer edge as you sew, using the full stretch of the bias. Using a clear open-toe foot and stitching slowly, topstitch the fabric just at the edge of the bias tape. Press the bias tape, stretching and relaxing the stretched outer edge.

You can use steam and starch to help relax and stretch the bias edge as needed so it lies flat.

If you stitch the inner curve first, don't allow it to stretch at all; save the stretch for the outer curved edge. Press the bias tape, stretching and relaxing the stretched outer edge before sewing it down.

If you are transitioning from an outer curve to an inner curve on the same seam or vice versa, you'll want to stretch along the outer curve and relax along the inner curve.

MAKE IT YOURS:
Designing a Unique Modern Medallion Quilt

While all the quilts in this book are designed as stand-alone projects, many of the center motifs and borders can be resized and mixed and matched. You can use the designs for the borders and center motifs exactly as written or as an inspiration as you put pencil to paper to create a quilt that is uniquely you! Don't rush it—enjoy the process. Designing projects almost always includes at least a bit of trial and error, but by taking your time, you can design and make a beautiful medallion quilt.

WHAT SIZE QUILT ARE YOU MAKING?

The first step in planning your modern medallion is to decide what size quilt you want to make. You don't need to decide the exact size, but are you making a pillow? A throw? A king? Here are some general ideas for sizes to get you started:

SIZE GUIDELINES

Wallhanging/pillow: 36″ × 36″ or smaller

Baby quilt: 45″ × 45″

Throw/lap quilt: 60″ × 60″

Bed quilts: Start with a square design equal to the smaller dimension for each bed size listed. Add borders to enlarge to a rectangular shape. Use one of the methods from Making a Border Fit (page 112) to find options for these additional borders. The amount of drop a quilt has (how far it hangs over the side of the bed) is a personal preference. For the most accurate sizing, take measurements of the intended bed using a tape measure.

    Twin: 65″ × 90″

    Full: 80″ × 90″

    Queen: 90″ × 100″

    King: 100″ × 100″

    California king: 96″ × 108″

CHOOSE OR DESIGN A CENTER MEDALLION

The best approach for making your own medallion is to begin with the center medallion or block and construct the quilt border by border, working your way out. You can choose a center medallion from the projects in this book, use a favorite block, or design your own. The traditional rule for the center medallion is to choose a design with a focal point and make it roughly one-quarter to one-third the size of your finished quilt. Whether you want to adhere to that rule is totally up to you. Some of the designers in this book followed that guideline, while others did not. Some of the designs include intricately pieced center medallions, which truly are the star of the quilt; other quilts include a simple center with the borders as the focal point; and still others are a combination of both. Play around with different ideas until you have a plan that makes you happy.

EXAMPLE: By varying the center block and choosing a different color palette, Karen Anderson-Abraham was able to dramatically change the look of her *Drop of Golden Sun* (page 29). She used a softer color palette, improv pieced the center in a Log Cabin style instead of a random one, and added more improv bits to the borders.

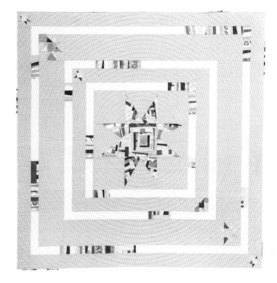

CHOOSE AND MAKE THE BORDERS

After you know what size quilt you are making and have made the center motif, it is time to work on the borders. If you are creating your own pattern or variation, you'll need to size them to fit either the center medallion or the previous border.

To start, measure your center medallion and choose your first border. If the border you choose is not the same size as the center, use one of the techniques in Making a Border Fit (page 112) to make it the desired size. The design of the border will determine which method will work best.

TWO IMPORTANT RULES TO FOLLOW AS YOU ADD BORDERS

- Always measure the quilt top through the middle as you plan your next border.

- When calculating the length of the next border, subtract the seam allowance from your overall measurement. Figure your calculations based on the "finished" measurement of your blocks and borders. After your calculations are done, add ¼" to each side for the seam allowance (a total of ½").

Making a Border Fit

Method 1: Add or Subtract Blocks from the Border

Many of the borders in this book are made up of small blocks, so it is easy to simply add or subtract blocks from the border to make it the size you need. This is easiest to do if your block measurement evenly divides into the border measurement.

> **Formula:** Length needed (finished border measurement or quilt width) × finished block width = number of blocks to make
>
> *Example: Need a 42″ border—42 × 6″ finished block width = 7 blocks*

If the number of blocks to make isn't a whole number (for example, it is 7.5), try Method 2: Resize the Blocks in the Border (below).

Method 2: Resize the Blocks in the Border

Several styles of border blocks, including Flying Geese, half-square triangles, and checkerboards, can be resized to fit the length needed.

If Method 1 doesn't give you a whole number:

Round the answer up or down to a whole number. Divide the length needed by the number of blocks until you get a size you can make.

> **Formula:** Length needed × rounded number of blocks = new finished size to make blocks
>
> *Example: If the quilt measures 38″ across the center and the original block is 5″, you would divide 38″ by 5″. However, that equals 7.6, which won't work! To find out what size will work, divide 38 by a whole number close to 7.6. So, 38 divided by 8 equals 4.75—that will work. Make 8 blocks that finish 4¾″ wide (5¼″ with seam allowances).*

When you know what size the blocks need to be, figure out how to make them that size. For Flying Geese blocks, use the instructions in Making Flying Geese (page 118) and follow the sizes given in the cutting charts (pages 119 and 121). For half-square triangles, use the instructions in Making Half-Square Triangles (page 123). If the border uses a template or foundation pattern, you can shrink or enlarge the pattern using a copy machine. This may take a little guesswork and a few tries to find the correct size. Other blocks can be redrafted with graph paper. Your extra efforts will be worth it in the end.

TIP: Before cutting fabrics for your entire border, make a sample block using scrap fabrics to check the measurements.

Method 3: Add an Element to the Border

If your block cannot be divided into the necessary border measurement, or if it is too complex for you to resize, you can add corner blocks (below), negative space (below), or center filler blocks (page 114).

These techniques are also great to use if you don't want to bother with resizing blocks or if you want to vary the way you resize and mix your borders.

METHOD 3A: ADD CORNER BLOCKS

Corner blocks are a great way to add interest to the quilt, and they make resizing and mixing borders easier. If you use corner blocks, you can simply make four identical borders instead of figuring out how to make all four borders join harmoniously. Further, you can use corner blocks to create a secondary design on your quilt, such as using differently sized but matching or coordinating corner blocks through the quilt to create a diagonal design. There are many possibilities of what to use for corner blocks: a solid square of fabric, a pieced block (as Erica used in *Oviedo Medallion*, page 45), or even an appliqué design (as Amy used in *ABC Medallion Wallhanging*, page 75).

METHOD 3B: ADD NEGATIVE SPACE TO THE BORDER

The medallion designs in this book are modern in nature, and several of the designs lend themselves to being asymmetrical and having negative space. You can simply make part or all of the desired border and then sew a strip of background fabric (or another fabric) to one or both short sides of the border or anywhere in between. You can make all four borders the same or vary them. Measure the quilt top as described in Choose and Make the Borders (page 111) and add fabric so the border is that measurement.

TIP: As Method 3B is very improvisational, it is best to work on a design wall so you can stand back and see your borders as you work.

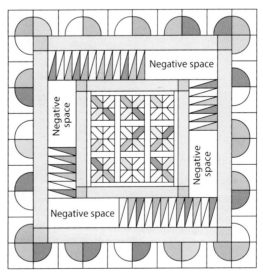

Negative space added to borders

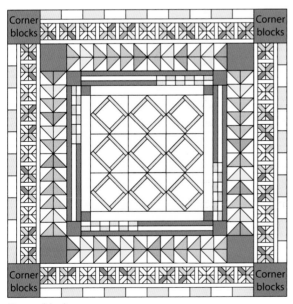

Corner blocks

METHOD 3C: ADD CENTER FILLER BLOCKS

Along the same idea as adding negative space to either side of a border, you can also add a block to the center of the border to make it fit. This block can be a piece of fabric, either a solid or print, which you can customize with appliqué, or you can make a simple block. Filler blocks take a little more planning than adding negative space to the end of a border.

Figure out how many complete blocks will fit in your border and determine their total *finished* length. Subtract that total length from the quilt measurement. Remember that you will probably want an equal number of blocks on each side of the center filler block.

Example: If your quilt is 38″ and your block is 4″ wide, you can fit 9.5 blocks. Round down to an even number of blocks: 8 blocks 4″ wide measure a total of 32″, which means you need a center filler block 6″ wide by the height of the border.

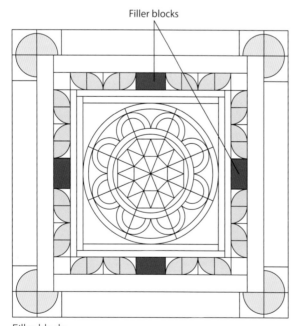
Filler blocks

Method 4: Add Filler Borders

Adding a plain filler border is a great way to make complex decorative borders fit. This is also a great technique to use if you've made a border and it is too big.

To figure out how wide to cut your filler borders, measure the quilt width (through the middle) and subtract it from the size of your *next pieced border*. The filler border width is half that measurement plus ½″ for seam allowance.

Formula: Next border – quilt width × 2 + ½″ = filler border width

Example: If your quilt is 38″ and your next border is 44″, your filler border should be 3½″ wide including seam allowance.

Filler borders

If you use filler borders, you might decide to customize them by doing one or more of the following:

- Use the bias tape appliqué technique as in *Zen Medallion* (page 103), or any of the other appliqué ideas in this book, to add an interesting design element to a plain border.

- Alternate between two solid colors for the plain border, as in *Migration Medallion* (page 15).

- Use a cheater or repeat print fabric, such as a chevron or stripes, to add visual interest to the plain borders, as in *One Step at a Time* (page 93).

- Use corner blocks in combination with your filler borders, as in *Alliance Medallion* (page 38).

MAKING A QUILT SMALLER

If you want to use one of the book's projects but need a smaller finished size, the simplest way to customize is to simply not make all of the borders. Just continue the project until you've reached the desired finished size. If you want to skip a border, use the instructions in Making a Border Fit on resizing the borders (page 112) to make the borders the size you need.

EXAMPLE: Beth interspersed borders from her *June Medallion* (page 53) with elements from other quilts in the book to make the pictured wallhanging. By combining her improv triangles with the Orange Peels (drawn freehand based on the pattern) from the *Wedding Bouquet Medallion* (page 63), the Flying Geese used throughout this book, and an abundance of negative space, she created a new look.

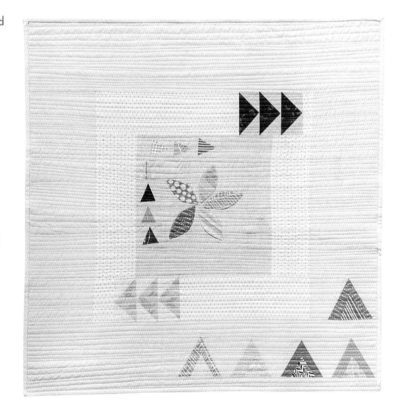

Other Ways to Use the Designs in This Book

While the designs in this book are primarily intended to help you make a modern medallion quilt, many of the center motifs and borders can be used in other types of quilts as well. Here are just some examples:

- Many of the center blocks and border blocks can be used as a block for a grid-based quilt. Use one of the blocks and repeat it several times, or mix together a few blocks for a sampler quilt.

- Make a quilt by repeating one more of the borders.

- Combine bits and pieces from a few of the quilts to make smaller projects. Many of the center blocks are a great size for a fun throw pillow, or you can use a center block plus one or two of the surrounding borders for a larger floor pillow or mini quilt. How about using three centers plus a border or two to create a table runner?

Feel free to use the projects in this book as a starting point. Let your imagination and creativity go to see what you can design!

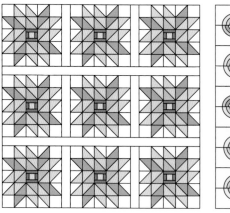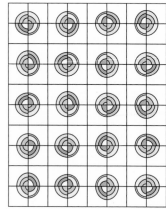

Center medallions and blocks in grid-based quilts

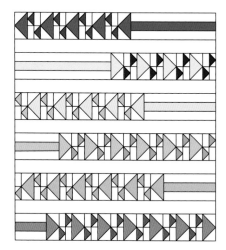

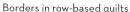

Borders in row-based quilts

SPECIAL TECHNIQUES

PIECING CURVES

Knowing how to piece curves will open up a whole new world of quilting designs. The most important thing to remember is to work slowly and pin liberally. You may be able to reduce your pin use with experience; just work at your own pace.

Pin the Curves

1. Take a look at the 2 pieces of fabric you will be sewing together: 1 piece will have a convex (curved-out) curve and the other a concave (curved-in, like the entrance to a cave) curve. *Figure A*

2. Fold each piece in half and crease to mark the center. Pin together the center points. *Figure B*

3. Pin together the corners and make sure they line up accurately. This will give you a nice, straight edge once your pieces are sewn together. *Figure C*

4. Continue pinning the edges and easing any extra fabric as needed. You may need to shift and repin in order to ease your fabric—but do not move the center pin. *Figure D*

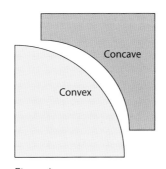

Figure A

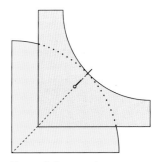

Figure B: Pin together centers.

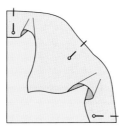

Figure C: Pin together corners.

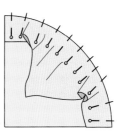

Figure D: Pinned curves

Sew the Curves

1. Sew together the pieces ¼" from the cut edge. You may need to flatten and stretch the fabric a bit with your left hand as you sew. Sew slowly and use the needle-down position on your machine so your pieces don't shift as you pivot. Remove the pins as you get to them and do not sew over them. Be sure to backstitch at the beginning and end of your seam.

TIP: It's usually easier to sew with the concave curve on top.

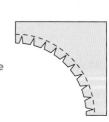

2. Press the seam allowance toward the concave curve. Because the seam allowance is ¼", you shouldn't need to clip the curves, but you can if necessary. We like to press lightly from the wrong side and then steam press from the right side, making sure the seam is flat and there are no puckers or folds. *Figure E*

TIP: Depending on the size of the curve, you may get a smoother seam if you clip the curved seam allowance after stitching.

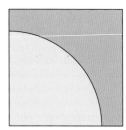

Figure E: Finished curve

MAKING FLYING GEESE

Flying Geese are a popular and versatile feature of medallion quilts. We are going to show you two ways to make Flying Geese. Which method is best for you depends on your personal preference, the number of geese needed, and whether you are using a fabric with a directional or nondirectional design.

IMPORTANT:

*In the instructions that follow, finished geese measurements do **not** include seam allowance.*

NOTE: True Flying Geese always follow the 2:1 rule—the width is twice the height.

One-at-a-Time Flying Geese

This method is great if you want an easy technique and are okay with wasting a bit of fabric. You can set up a whole stack and chain piece (page 13) one side and then prep and chain piece the other side. It is ideal when using directional prints.

1. Cut a rectangle that is ½" longer and ½" wider that the desired size of the finished Flying Geese block. (Example: If the finished block is to be 4" × 2", cut the rectangle 4½" × 2½".)

2. Cut 2 squares the height of the rectangle. (Example: Cut 2 squares 2½" × 2½".)

3. Draw a diagonal line on the wrong side of each square. *Figure F*

4. Place a square on the rectangle, right sides together, aligning outer corners and edges. Sew on the marked diagonal line. *Figure G*

5. Trim off the corner, leaving a ¼" seam allowance. Press toward the background triangle. *Figure H*

6. Repeat Steps 4 and 5 on the opposite side of the rectangle to complete the unit. *Figure I*

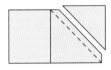

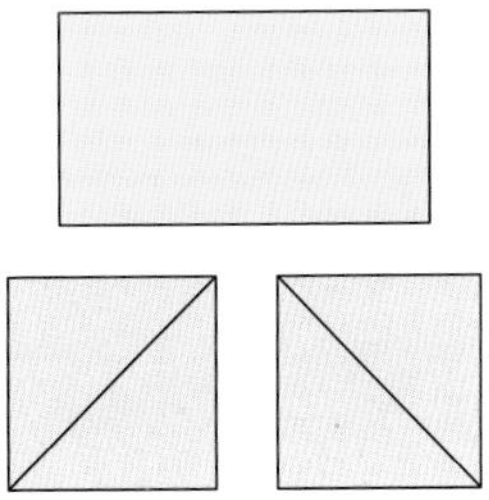

Figure F   Figure G

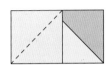

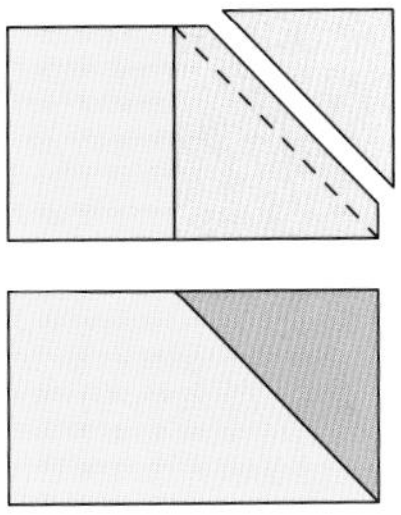

Figure H 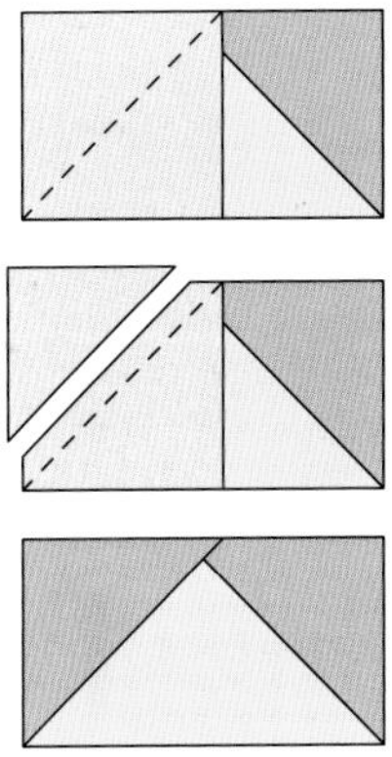   Figure I: Finished!

Cutting for One-at-a-Time Flying Geese

FINISHED SIZE	RECTANGLE SIZE: (Formula: finished size plus ½")	SQUARE SIZE: (Formula: finished height plus ½")
¾" × 1½"	1¼" × 2"	1¼" × 1¼"
1" × 2"	1½" × 2½"	1½" × 1½"
1¼" × 2½"	1¾" × 3"	1¾" × 1¾"
1½" × 3"	2" × 3½"	2" × 2"
1¾" × 3½"	2¼" × 4"	2¼" × 2¼"
2" × 4"	2½" × 4½"	2½" × 2½"
2¼" × 4½"	2¾" × 5"	2¾" × 2¾"
2½" × 5"	3" × 5½"	3" × 3"
2¾" × 5½"	3¼" × 6"	3¼" × 3¼"
3" × 6"	✓ 3½" × 6½"	✓ 3½" × 3½"
3¼" × 6½"	3¾" × 7"	3¾" × 3¾"
3½" × 7"	4" × 7½"	4" × 4"
3¾" × 7½"	4¼" × 8"	4¼" × 4¼"
4" × 8"	4½" × 8½"	4½" × 4½"

Four-at-a-Time Flying Geese

This method is efficient and creates zero waste. Once you learn it, you'll feel like you are performing a little bit of magic. The one drawback is that directional prints will face different directions on each of the four geese. While this is not desirable in many quilts, it can be a fun design feature if you are making an entire border of Flying Geese.

1. Cut a square with all sides equaling the finished *width* of the Flying Geese + 1¼". *Figure J*

2. Cut 4 smaller squares equaling the finished *height* of the Flying Geese + ⅞". Draw a diagonal line from corner to corner on the wrong side of the small squares. *Figure J*

3. Pin 2 small squares, right sides together, at 2 opposite corners of the large square. Align the marked lines as shown. The corners of the small squares will overlap a tiny bit. Sew on either side of the line with a scant ¼" seam allowance. *Figure K*

4. Cut the squares in half on the marked line. *Figure L*

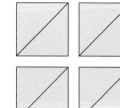

Figure J

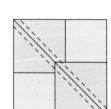

Figure K

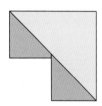

Figure L

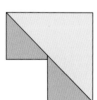

Figure M

5. Flip the fabric open along the seam. Press the seam allowances toward the small triangles. *Figure M*

6. Pin a small square, right sides together, on top of each large triangle. Sew on either side of the line with a scant ¼″ seam. *Figure N*

7. Cut apart along the drawn line. Press triangles open, with the seam allowances toward the small triangles.

You now have four Flying Geese! *Figure O*

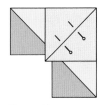
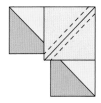
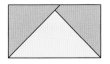

Figure N

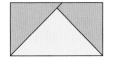
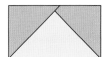

Figure O

Cutting for Four-at-a-Time Flying Geese

FINISHED GEESE SIZE	LARGE SQUARE: (Formula: finished width + 1¼″)	SMALL SQUARES (CUT 4): (Formula: finished height + ⅞″)
¾″ × 1½″	2¾″ × 2¾″	1⅝″ × 1⅝″
1″ × 2″	3¼″ × 3¼″	1⅞″ × 1⅞″
1¼″ × 2½″	3¾″ × 3¾″	2⅛″ × 2⅛″
1½″ × 3″	4¼″ × 4¼″	2⅜″ × 2⅜″
1¾″ × 3½″	4¾″ × 4¾″	2⅝″ × 2⅝″
2″ × 4″	5¼″ × 5¼″	2⅞″ × 2⅞″
2¼″ × 4½″	5¾″ × 5¾″	3⅛″ × 3⅛″
2½″ × 5″	6¼″ × 6¼″	3⅜″ × 3⅜″
2¾″ × 5½″	6¾″ × 6¾″	3⅝″ × 3⅝″
3″ × 6″	7¼″ × 7¼″	3⅞″ × 3⅞″
3¼″ × 6½″	7¾″ × 7¾″	4⅛″ × 4⅛″
3½″ × 7″	8¼″ × 8¼″	4⅜″ × 4⅜″
3¾″ × 7½″	8¾″ × 8¾″	4⅝″ × 4⅝″
4″ × 8″	9¼″ × 9¼″	4⅞″ × 4⅞″

Truing Up Flying Geese

Your Flying Geese are made, and it's time to piece them together. Are the edges of your geese perfectly straight? Probably not, because you have been sewing bias seams, and they tend to stretch a little during sewing and pressing. *Figure P*

To true up the edges of your geese, use a quilter's ruler with a 45° angle. *Make sure not to trim down so much that your finished units are smaller than intended.*

1. Line up the ruler so that the 45° line is on top of a diagonal seamline and the ¼" line intersects the point. Trim the background edge of the unit. *Figure Q*

2. Trim the opposite edge of your Flying Geese to the intended height. Make sure the ruler stays parallel to the already-trimmed edge of the unit. *Figure R*

3. To trim the right-hand side, place the 45° line on the right diagonal seam and align the midpoint measurement of your Flying Geese with the point. (Example: If you are making a 2" × 4" unit, it will be 4½" wide with seam allowance; so the midpoint would be 2¼" on your ruler.) *Figure S*

4. Measure and trim the left-hand side to the intended width. Make sure the ruler stays parallel to the opposite side. *Figure T*

TIP: If you find that your edges are ⅛" or more off or for really accurate geese, make your Flying Geese a size larger and trim them down to the size you want them to be.

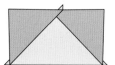

Figure P: Flying Geese with uneven edges

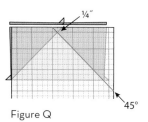

Figure Q

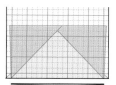

Figure R

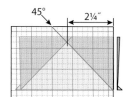

Figure S

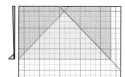

Figure T

MAKING HALF-SQUARE TRIANGLES

Refer to the project instructions for the size of the squares. In general, your cut size should be 7⁄8" larger than your finished size.

> **TIP:** Cutting your squares about 1⁄8" larger than the instructions indicate will make it easier to trim them to the needed finished size, but it will produce more waste. Try it both ways and see which you prefer.

1. With right sides together, pair 2 squares. Use your preferred fabric-marking tool to draw a diagonal line from a corner to the opposite corner on the wrong sides of a square.

2. Sew a scant 1⁄4" on each side of the line. *Figure U*

Figure U

> **TIP:** If you will be sewing several half-square triangles, try pairing the squares together as directed in the project instructions and then chain piecing (page 13) them. You can sew down one side of the line for all of your squares and then flip the pile and sew down the other side, without clipping the threads until you have sewn both sides.

Figure V

3. Cut on the drawn line. *Figure V*

4. Press and trim to the size stated in the project. Use the 45° diagonal line on your quilting ruler or cutting mat to help square your half-square triangles. *Figure W*

Figure W: Finished!

FOUNDATION PAPER PIECING

Foundation paper piecing is a technique in which the fabrics are sewn in numerical order to a (usually) paper pattern that serves as a temporary foundation. Paper piecing is a great way to create designs with perfect points, without the stress of matching those points and fiddling with small pieces. As with any new technique, take your time—you'll be a pro in no time.

Tips for Foundation Paper Piecing

- Use paper designed specifically for foundation paper piecing, such as Carol Doak's Foundation Paper or Simple Foundations Translucent Vellum Paper. You can also try copy paper.

- Write the colors of your fabric directly onto your pattern or use colored pencils to color in your foundation pattern for reference when sewing.

- Shorten your stitch length to about 1.5, or about 17–19 stitches per inch.

- Place fabrics on the unprinted side of the foundation pattern and sew on the printed side.

- Press with a dry iron after sewing each seam.

- Backstitch in the seam allowance at the beginning and end of each seam. This will keep your stitches from getting loose when you tear off the papers.

- Begin with piece number 1 on your paper pattern; then piece in numerical order.

- When you are just learning to paper piece, it helps to use larger pieces of fabric so you have more wiggle room for errors. Allow at least ½" extra on each side. It will be more wasteful, but as you master the technique, you can cut your fabric pieces smaller.

Prepare the Fabrics and Patterns

1. Copy as many foundation patterns as you will need. Make sure your copies are the same size and are not distorted. Cut them out along the outer dashed seam allowance line. Cut the needed fabrics according to the directions in the project.

2. Take a look at your foundation pattern. It is a mirror image of the finished piece. The solid black lines are the stitching lines, and the numbers indicate the order in which the fabric will be placed and sewn. *Figure X*

> **TIP:** If you use thin or translucent paper, you will easily be able to see the printed lines on the reverse side of the template. If you have trouble seeing the lines, crease the pattern along the sewing lines, use a tracing wheel to perforate the paper, or simply hold it up to the light as you place the fabric.

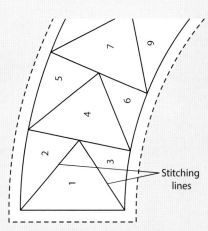

Figure X: Foundation pattern with stitching lines

Sew

1. Pin the first piece of fabric, right side up, on space 1 of the unprinted side of the foundation pattern.

> **IMPORTANT:** Only the first piece of fabric is placed right side up. Every piece sewn after that will be wrong side up.

Make sure the edges of the fabric extend at least 1/4" past the borders of space 1. If you prefer, you can use a glue stick instead of pins. *Figure Y*

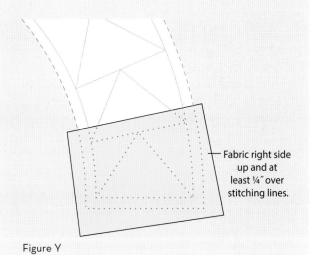

Fabric right side up and at least 1/4" over stitching lines.

Figure Y

2. Pin the piece for space 2, right sides together, on top of piece 1 as shown. It should be parallel to the stitching line between spaces 1 and 2. Check that piece 2 will cover the entire area and overlap by ¼″ or more on all sides when it is flipped. If you are worried, sew with a basting stitch first, flip and check the placement. *Figure Z*

3. Make sure your machine is back to a short stitch length. With the printed side up, sew on the stitching line. *Figure AA*

4. Fold back the foundation pattern on the stitching line. Trim the seam allowances to ¼″, using a ruler and rotary cutter or just using scissors and simply eyeballing a ¼″ seam allowance. Flip piece 2 open and gently press flat. *Figure BB*

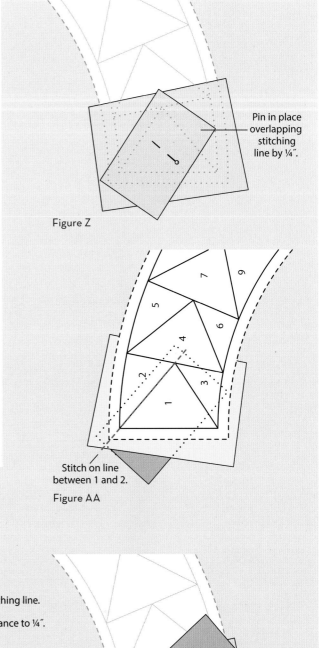

Pin in place overlapping stitching line by ¼″.

Figure Z

Stitch on line between 1 and 2.

Figure AA

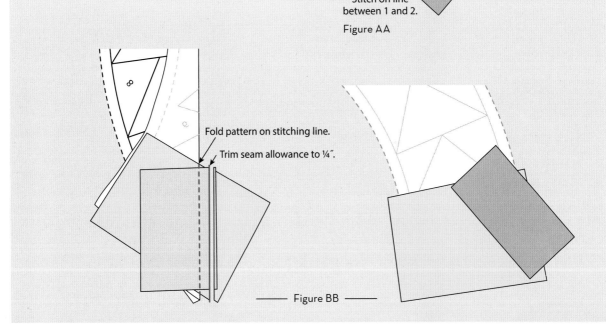

Fold pattern on stitching line.

Trim seam allowance to ¼″.

Figure BB

5. Repeat Steps 2–4, following the numbers on the foundation pattern, until you have pieced the entire foundation. *Figures CC & DD*

6. Trim the outer edge of the entire foundation pattern, leaving ¼" seam allowances. *Figure EE*

7. Gently remove the paper and press again if needed. Your paper piecing is complete.

TIP: To make your sewing time more efficient, set up cutting and ironing stations near your sewing machine.

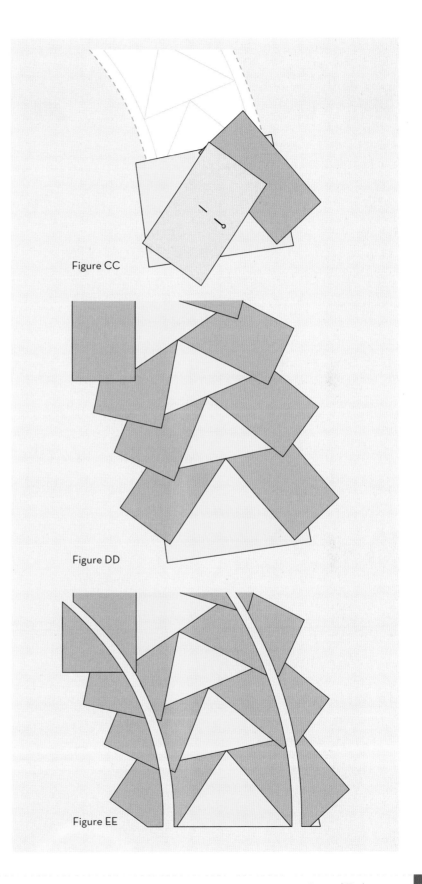

Figure CC

Figure DD

Figure EE

Migration Medallion (page 15) by Janice Zeller Ryan

Watch the Birdie (page 23) by Kerry Green

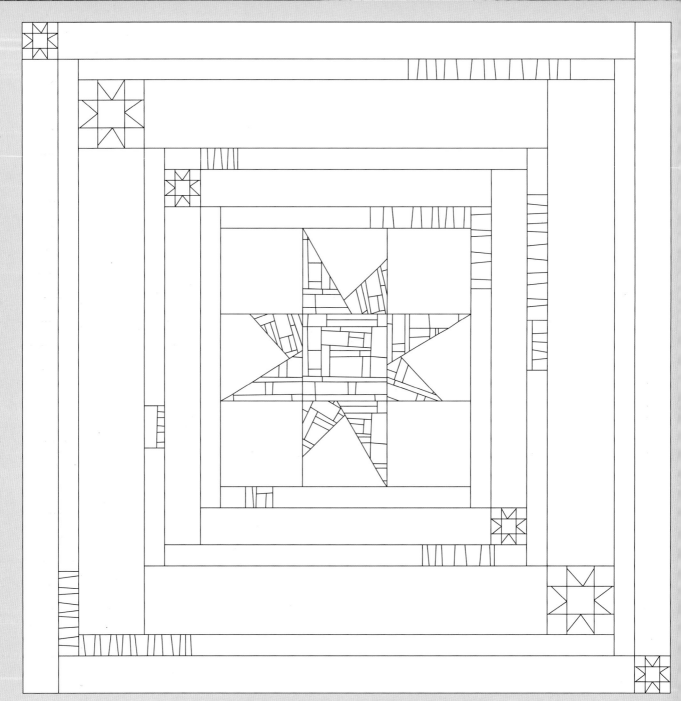

Drop of Golden Sun (page 29) by Karen Anderson-Abraham

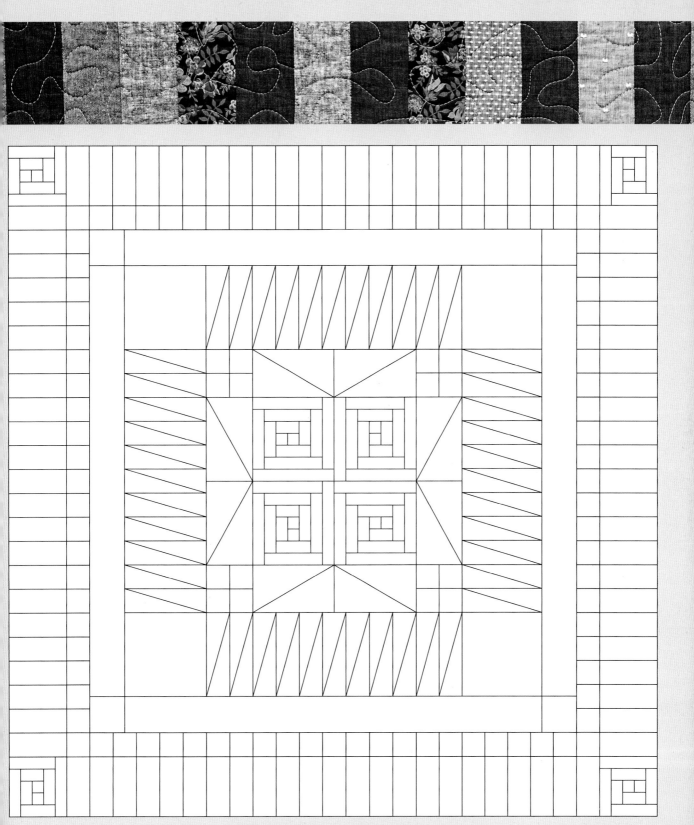

Alliance Medallion (page 38) by Alexia Marcelle Abegg

Oviedo Medallion (page 45) by Erica Jackman

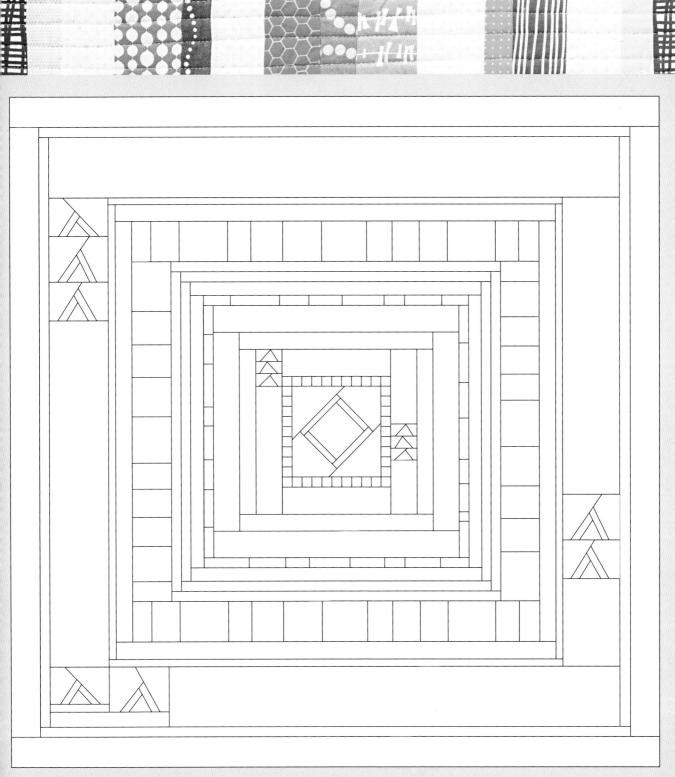

June Medallion (page 53) by Beth Vassalo

Wedding Bouquet Medallion (page 63) by Rebecca Bryan

ABC Medallion Wallhanging (page 75) by Amy Sinibaldi

Graphical Modern Medallion (page 81) by Christina Lane

One Step at a Time (page 93) by Melissa Richie

Zen Medallion (page 103) by Latifah Saafir

ABOUT THE CONTRIBUTORS

ALEXIA MARCELLE ABEGG

Alexia Marcelle Abegg was born in Folsom, California, on the day Mount St. Helens erupted. Always fascinated with the art of sewing, Alexia grew up watching her mother create everything from bridal gowns to costumes. She studied fashion and fine arts in college. After trying her hand at photography, production, acting, costuming, hair and makeup for film and television, fashion design, and custom sewing, she found her home in creating fine art quilts and sewing patterns while living in Brooklyn, New York, and working at The City Quilter.

Alexia and her husband, artist and fabric designer Rob Bancroft, live in Nashville with their two dogs, Soda and Olive. She currently divides her time among creating patterns for their company, Green Bee Design and Patterns; teaching; making art; designing fabric for Cotton + Steel; and writing. She is the author of *Liberty Love* and has contributed to many books and magazines. Visit her at alexiaabegg.squarespace.com.

KAREN ANDERSON-ABRAHAM

Karen has always had a deep love and appreciation for art, textiles, and crafts. With a strong desire to create beauty, warmth, and comfort after the birth of her first child, she eagerly began her quiltmaking journey. She enjoys composing small abstract pieces as well as more traditional bed quilts with a modern twist. She is inspired by the colors and textures of her natural environment, modern art and architecture, and traditional and modern patterns in fabrics and textiles from around the world. She considers herself a perpetual student of craft and design, whose creative aesthetic is continually changing and growing—from ultra modern and clean on one hand to charming and sweet on the other—but always with fresh and interesting design elements. She loves clean lines; sophisticated, subtle color palettes; and an abundance of negative space. However, the influence of her young daughters often inspires her to create charming pieces with sweet, fresh infusions of color. She is honored to have had a number of her quilts accepted into both national and international quilt shows. Karen writes about her quilting process at bloomingpoppies.net.

REBECCA BRYAN

As a fourth-generation quilter, Rebecca grew up in a family of makers. Her lovely mother graciously taught Rebecca everything she knew about sewing and helped Rebecca make her first official quilt for her first official apartment. Rebecca has been quilting passionately ever since.

Once upon a time, Rebecca taught high school, earned a master's degree, and worked in research. Back then she found her creative outlet in embroidery and quiltmaking. These days every bit of Rebecca's education and mental energy goes toward raising her young children—as only a perfectionist and overachiever would—but she still finds her creative outlet in designing and making quilts.

She is the author of *Modern Rainbow: 14 Imaginative Quilts That Play with Color* (Stash Books). Rebecca lives in Houston, Texas, with her husband, four children, and two dogs. You can find out more about Rebecca and her quilts by visiting her blog, www.bryanhousequilts.com.

KERRY GREEN

Kerry loves thrifty finds, vintage fabric, and sewing in all its forms—quilting, zakka, dressmaking—she wants to sew it all! She shares tips, patterns, and tutorials at her personal blog. Through the online community she met Penny Layman, and together they formed Sew-Ichigo, where they combine graphic, vintage-inspired ideas to make paper-piecing and quilt block patterns. Kerry is co-author of *500 Quilt Blocks* (Search Press); she has also been published in *Playful Little Paper-Pieced Projects* (Stash Books).

Kerry keeps two blogs: verykerryberry.blogspot.com and sew-ichigo.blogspot.com.

ERICA JACKMAN

Erica lives in San Diego, California, with her husband and two wonderful children. She is a self-taught quilter with a serious love for fabric. During college she studied biology and  creative writing, and she loves that quilting satisfies both the left and right side of her brain. But most of all she enjoys making sure that none of her friends or family will ever be cold again. When she isn't quilting, Erica loves to read, spend time with her family, and wander aimlessly around Target. You can find her online at kitchentablequilting.blogspot.com.

CHRISTINA LANE

Christina is a professional longarm quilter and pattern designer residing in the beautiful Pacific Northwest. She co-authored *Quilting Happiness* and has contributed to many  publications over the years. Find out more about Christina at sometimescrafter.com.

MELISSA RICHIE

Melissa first dabbled in quilting in 1997, but she didn't realize her passion for it until 2009, when she discovered modern quilting. She joined the Los Angeles Modern  Quilt Guild and found a group of like-minded quilters who inspired, encouraged, and challenged her and shared their love of beautiful fabric with her. After a few short months, she moved to Colorado Springs and founded the Front Range Modern Quilt Guild, where she served as president for three years. She is currently pursuing her dreams of quilt design, longarm quilting, and making quilts for charity. Melissa and her husband are active in their local church, and she donates many quilts to a local charity. Melissa feels very blessed to be married to a patient and supportive man and to be able to stay home and raise their two daughters and one son. Melissa blogs at weshallsew.blogspot.com.

LATIFAH SAAFIR

Sewing has been Latifah Saafir's portal to creativity ever since she "took it up seriously" at the age of eleven. Having learned the basics at the knee of her mother at age six, she focused on sewing garments throughout her teenage years and through college, eventually sewing much of her own wardrobe. A mechanical engineer by training, she took classes in design "to keep her sanity." In search of a new avenue for her creativity, Latifah discovered quilting in 2009, and just a few months later, with only one quilt under her belt, she co-founded the Modern Quilt Guild. She quickly transferred her sewing skills to quilting as she created more than twenty quilts in her first year.

Latifah is known for her bold use of color and innovative design. She teaches her innovative techniques and is excited to be working on her first series of quilt patterns and products. She blogs about her quilting adventures at thequiltengineer.com.

AMY SINIBALDI

Amy lives in Los Angeles in a small house by the ocean. She sews, designs, and blogs about her creative life while tending four children, a husband, and a wildly overflowing craft corner stuffed with fabric and notions. She is a contributor to several books and magazines, runs a small Etsy shop, and offers many simple and easy sewing tutorials on her blog. With her children as inspiration, Amy creates handmade goods with a desire to add extra touches of charm into their lives—and the lives of others. Find Amy online at nanacompany.typepad.com.

ABOUT THE AUTHORS

JANICE ZELLER RYAN

Janice has been a long-time addict of all things fabric and sewing. She began her career designing and sewing costumes for theater, and she holds a master of fine arts in costume design from Carnegie Mellon University. The birth of her children (and the creation of her first baby quilt) took her in a new direction, where she discovered her love of quilting. Janice is a member of the Los Angeles Modern Quilt Guild, and she teaches classes in quilting and garment sewing at Sew Modern in Los Angeles. You can find tips, patterns, and tutorials on her blog betteroffthread.com.

BETH VASSALO

Beth was inspired to learn how to use a sewing machine about seven years ago while watching her young daughter create dress-up clothes and accessories using just paper and tape. With the help of several books and online sources, Beth learned the basics and was soon regularly sewing, knitting, and crocheting projects for herself and her three daughters. A few years later, Beth discovered quilting and has been designing and making quilts ever since. Beth shares her sewing adventures at plumandjune.blogspot.com.